By the
NuMbErs
3.14

By the Numbers 3.14

NATIONAL GEOGRAPHIC KiDS

WASHINGTON, D.C.

What is an INFOGRAPHIC?
And what's this book ALL ABOUT?

Get ready to see numbers in a totally new way! *By the Numbers 3.14* is all about bringing facts and figures to life so you can understand the stories behind the data. You won't find pages of boring old numbers in this book. Instead, you'll see them in stunning photos, cool illustrations, fun graphs, and wild charts. How'd we do it? When you combine the powers of *information* and *graphics*, you get *infographics*!

These innovative graphics turn confusing numbers into a quick, fun way to learn all sorts of different facts about animals, nature, science, and more. Infographics come in many different shapes, sizes, patterns, and colors, and you'll see them all in this book. So prepare to be wowed, surprised, and totally amazed. You're about to see numbers, data, and statistics like you've never seen them before.

Infographics in this book:

PHOTO INFOGRAPHICS
These infographics use incredible photos to visualize numbers and data, while pop-ups reveal the facts behind the figures. See pages 14–15 and 112–113.

WORD CLOUDS
What's a word cloud? Exactly what it sounds like—a cloud of words, where each word's size is different. Word clouds show the concept of frequency in math and statistics—bigger numbers (and words!) are more important. See pages 92–93.

MAPS
Where in the world is a fact located? Check the map! Look for location markers to help you discover the exact location of different data points. See pages 126–127 and 174–175.

PIE CHARTS

Hungry for a piece of pie? This type of chart can show you lots of information about numbers. Each section of the pie represents a percentage of the whole. Dig in!

See pages 6–7 and 74–75.

VISUAL ARTICLES

If the subject is super complicated, a visual article can break it down for you! Visual articles are infographics that turn big ideas with lots of information into a simple visual story that you can easily understand.

See pages 86–87 and 200–201.

VERSUS OR COMPARISON INFOGRAPHICS

Time for a showdown! In a comparison infographic, we'll put two or more things side by side so we can see their similarities and differences.

See pages 48–49 and 232–233.

GRAPHS

These graphs may look familiar, but these aren't the boring bar charts you've seen in school! See how we've snazzed up these classic charts.

See pages 56–57 and 132–133.

BUBBLE CHARTS

Bubble charts show stats in the form of circles or other shapes, where the biggest bubbles represent the biggest numbers. Comparing the size of the bubbles can show you the differences between the data points.

See pages 46–47 and 110–111.

TIMELINES

Like a calendar of important dates, these infographics are organized chronologically to tell a story from start to finish.

See pages 62–63 and 182–183.

Meet the EXPERTS!

IN *BY THE NUMBERS 3.14*, YOU'LL ALSO MEET FASCINATING PEOPLE WORKING IN THE FIELD OF MATH AND NUMBERS. GET REAL ADVICE ON MATH, SCIENCE, AND HOW TO BECOME A STATISTICS STAR. PLUS, LEARN EXACTLY HOW THESE EXPERTS ARE CHANGING THE WORLD WITH THE POWER OF NUMBERS!

DELICIOUS DOUGHNUT DATA

Whether they're glazed, iced, sprinkled, or filled, doughnuts are loved by people around the world! Researchers surveyed 735 people in the United States to find out their favorite flavors. Get ready to be a-glazed! Er ... amazed!

5.3%
OTHER

7.6%
PLAIN

9.7%
FROSTED WITH SPRINKLES

12.9%
JELLY FILLED

26.3%
GLAZED

20.8%
CHOCOLATE

17.4%
CUSTARD FILLED

FREQUENT **FLYERS**

Air travel is the quickest way to get from here to there. Every day, more than 8 million people around the world take a trip on an airplane. That's a lot of travelers! So where are most people passing through? Here's a look at the world's busiest airports.

76,942,493
ANNUAL PASSENGERS

👤👤👤👤👤👤👤👤👤👤

O'HARE INTERNATIONAL AIRPORT (ORD)
Where: Chicago, Illinois, U.S.A.

101,491,106
ANNUAL PASSENGERS

👤👤👤👤👤👤👤👤👤👤👤

HARTSFIELD-JACKSON ATLANTA INTERNATIONAL AIRPORT (ATL)
Where: Atlanta, Georgia, U.S.A.

WINNER! Hartsfield-Jackson Atlanta International Airport has been the world's busiest airport every year since 2000.

39,213,865
ANNUAL PASSENGERS

👤👤👤👤

SÃO PAULO–GUARULHOS INTERNATIONAL AIRPORT (GRU)
Where: Guarulhos, São Paulo, Brazil

74,989,795
ANNUAL PASSENGERS
👤👤👤👤👤👤👤👤

**LONDON HEATHROW
AIRPORT** (LHR)
Where: Hillingdon, London, United Kingdom

89,938,628
ANNUAL PASSENGERS
👤👤👤👤👤👤👤👤👤

**BEIJING CAPITAL
INTERNATIONAL AIRPORT** (PEK)
Where: Chaoyang-Shunyi, Beijing, China

78,014,841
ANNUAL PASSENGERS
👤👤👤👤👤👤👤👤

**DUBAI INTERNATIONAL
AIRPORT** (DXB)
Where: Garhoud, Dubai, United Arab Emirates

 = 10,000,000 PEOPLE

AMPELOSAURUS, A 50-FOOT (15-M)-LONG DINOSAUR, HAD A TINY BRAIN WITH A VOLUME OF

1.3 OUNCES

(39.5 cm³)

WHO ARE YOU CALLING WALNUT BRAIN?
I LIVED 70 MILLION YEARS AGO. I'M OLD ENOUGH TO BE YOUR GREAT-GREAT-GREAT- ... I FORGET. WHAT ARE WE TALKING ABOUT AGAIN?

THAT'S THE SIZE OF A

WALNUT!

SUPERHERO STATS

Calling all comic fans! Sure, you've read pretty much all of the Superman comics and seen the Avengers movies more times than you can count. But do you know the numbers behind your favorite superpowered protagonists? It's time to put on your thinking cape—er, cap—and find out!

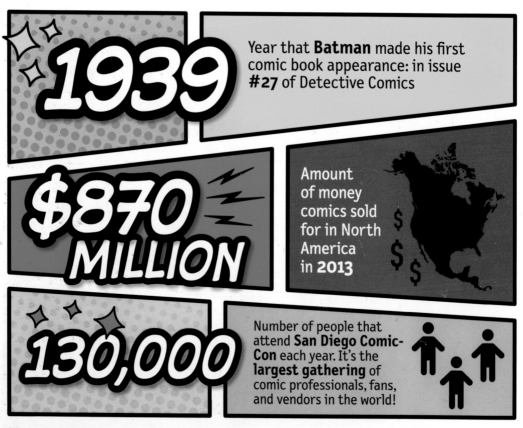

1939
Year that **Batman** made his first comic book appearance: in issue **#27** of Detective Comics

$870 MILLION
Amount of money comics sold for in North America in **2013**

130,000
Number of people that attend **San Diego Comic-Con** each year. It's the **largest gathering** of comic professionals, fans, and vendors in the world!

$3.2 MILLION

Winning bid on a near-perfect copy of Action Comics **#1,** making it the only comic to have sold for more than **$3 million.** This issue features the first appearance of **Superman!**

232

Number of characters on the cover of Deadpool **#27**—setting **a world record** for most characters ever featured on a comic book cover!

358

Number of comic book characters created or co-created by **Stan Lee,** Marvel's famous comic writer, editor, and publisher.

$623 MILLION

Amount of money earned from ticket sales for Marvel's **2012** movie version of *The Avengers,* making it the most successful comic book movie of all time.

Did you know that starfish aren't really fish? They're invertebrates! That means these critters, more accurately called sea stars, don't have backbones like fish do. Check out these fun sea star stats.

DIET:
CLAMS, OYSTERS, AND SNAILS

ARMS:
MOST HAVE 5
BUT SOME SPECIES, LIKE *HELICOILASTER*, CAN HAVE UP TO 50!

SIZE:

4.7–9.4 INCHES
(12–24 CM)

The biggest starfish species, *Pycnopodia helianthoides*, can grow up to **31 INCHES (80 cm)** in diameter!

LIFE SPAN:
UP TO 35 YEARS

WEIGHT:
UP TO 11 POUNDS
(5 KG)

DEPTH:
UP TO 20,000 FEET
(6,000 M)

SUPER SPELLERS

In 1925, a group of 9 newspapers had a bright idea. They wanted to make spelling, a "dull subject," more fun for kids. Their solution? Turn it into a game! During the Scripps National Spelling Bee, kids from around the country compete to spell harder and harder words, with the winner being crowned the Spelling Bee champion. Dust off your dictionary and check out these Bee basics.

285
NUMBER OF KIDS WHO COMPETED IN THE 2016 BEE

24.5%
PERCENT OF 2016 COMPETITORS WHO HAD ENTERED BEFORE

6
AGE OF YOUNGEST SPELLER

66.6%

PERCENT OF 2016 SPELLERS WHO WENT TO PUBLIC SCHOOL

MORE THAN 472,000
NUMBER OF WORDS IN *WEBSTER'S THIRD NEW INTERNATIONAL DICTIONARY,* THE OFFICIAL DICTIONARY OF THE SPELLING BEE

Winning word for the 1925 Spelling Bee: GLADIOLUS | Winning words for the 2016 Spelling Bee: FELDENKRAIS and GESELLSCHAFT

4
NUMBER OF TIMES 2
PEOPLE HAVE WON
THE SPELLING BEE,
INCLUDING 2016

2 MINUTES
AMOUNT OF TIME KIDS ARE
GIVEN TO SPELL A WORD

1994
FIRST YEAR THE
SPELLING BEE WAS
BROADCAST ON ESPN

1821

Here's a study tip! The word CONNOISSEUR is the most frequent word on the Spelling Bee word list.

THE BIG PICTURE

Say cheese! Thanks to new camera technology, we're taking more photos now than ever before. In fact, the number has tripled since 2010! Look at the chart below to see just how many snapshots people are taking.

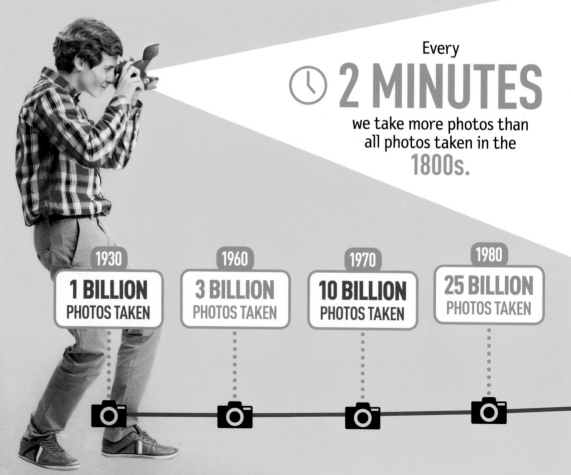

Every

2 MINUTES

we take more photos than all photos taken in the **1800s.**

1930
1 BILLION
PHOTOS TAKEN

1960
3 BILLION
PHOTOS TAKEN

1970
10 BILLION
PHOTOS TAKEN

1980
25 BILLION
PHOTOS TAKEN

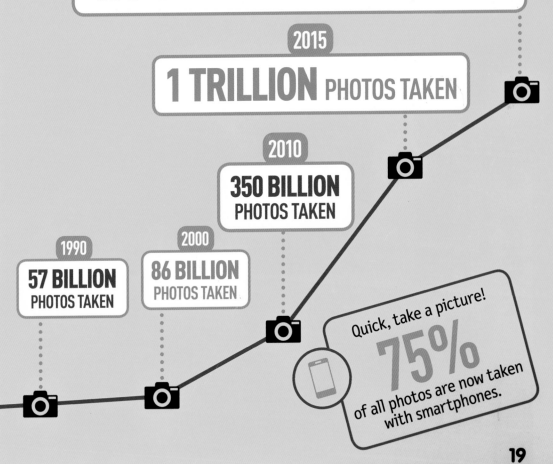

2017

1.3 TRILLION (ESTIMATED) PHOTOS TAKEN

2015

1 TRILLION PHOTOS TAKEN

2010

350 BILLION PHOTOS TAKEN

1990

57 BILLION PHOTOS TAKEN

2000

86 BILLION PHOTOS TAKEN

Quick, take a picture!

75%
of all photos are now taken with smartphones.

CELL PHONE NUMBERS

91% of Americans own a mobile phone. What is everyone doing with their screen time? Dial in to find out the most popular activities people do on their phones.

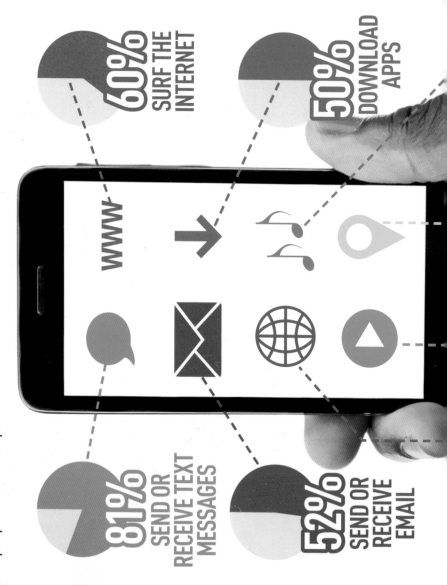

60% SURF THE INTERNET

50% DOWNLOAD APPS

81% SEND OR RECEIVE TEXT MESSAGES

52% SEND OR RECEIVE EMAIL

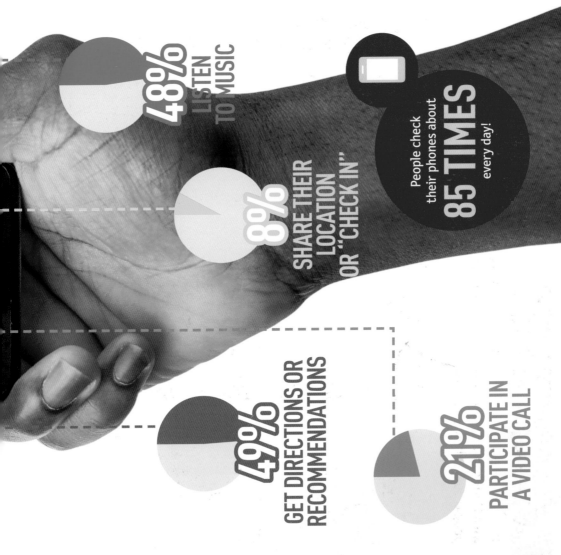

48%
LISTEN TO MUSIC

8%
SHARE THEIR LOCATION OR "CHECK IN"

People check their phones about **85 TIMES** every day!

49%
GET DIRECTIONS OR RECOMMENDATIONS

21%
PARTICIPATE IN A VIDEO CALL

ON THE **FAST TRACK**

All aboard the fastest passenger train in the world!
This special train doesn't even touch the tracks as it carries people to the airport in Shanghai, China. Maglev trains use the power of magnets to lift and propel the train cars forward for a smooth, superfast ride. Here are some fast facts about this speed train!

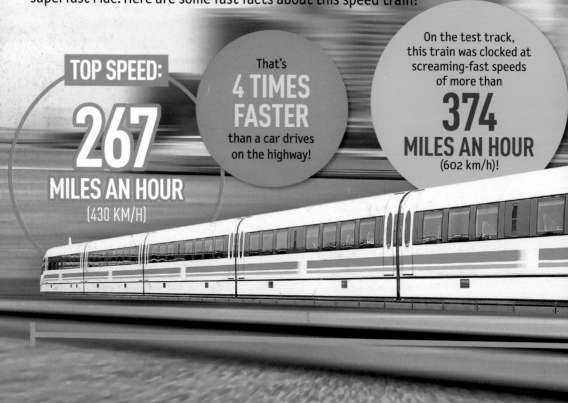

TOP SPEED:

267
MILES AN HOUR
(430 KM/H)

That's
4 TIMES FASTER
than a car drives on the highway!

On the test track, this train was clocked at screaming-fast speeds of more than

374
MILES AN HOUR
(602 km/h)!

NUMBER OF PASSENGERS:

574

WIDTH:

12 FEET

(3.7 M)

That's wider than
2 CARS
side by side!

The Shanghai Maglev Train cost
$1.2 BILLION
to build!

LENGTH:

502 FEET

(153 M)

That's longer than
10 SEMI-TRUCKS!

ANIMAL **ASTRONAUTS**

Can you imagine a dog flying into outer space? It really happened, and lots of other animals have been in space, too. Ever since spaceflight was first developed in the 1940s, all kinds of animals have been passengers on rockets in the name of science. Here's a look at some of these historic animal astronauts.

JUNE 4,
1949

Albert II was the first **MONKEY** in space, reaching a height of **83 MILES** (134 KM). Since then, a total of **32 MONKEYS** have flown in space.

FEBRUARY 20,
1947

The first animals in outer space were very small ones: **FRUIT FLIES!** The flies launched **68 MILES** (108 KM) into the atmosphere before parachuting back down to Earth.

NOVEMBER 3,
1957

LAIKA THE DOG was a true pioneer! As a passenger on **SPUTNIK 2**, she was the first living creature to orbit the Earth.

1973

Two **SPIDERS** spin webs on NASA's Skylab space station for **59 DAYS**.

2013

MICE spend a month on the **BION-M1 SPACECRAFT** experiencing life in space.

JULY 2, 1959

The first **RABBIT** launches into space, along with **2 DOGS**.

OCTOBER 18, 1963

Félicette becomes the first **CAT** in space, flying **100 MILES** (160 KM) high.

VEGETABLES: **5 DAYS–1 MONTH**

PAPER: **2–5 MONTHS**

COTTON T-SHIRTS: **6 MONTHS**

TREE LEAVES: **1 YEAR**

PLASTIC-COATED PAPER MILK CARTONS: **5 YEARS**

ALUMINUM CANS: **80–100 YEARS**

Next time you have a soda, don't toss that can. Recycle it! From the time you recycle a can, it takes only 60 days to turn it into a new one. Compare that with the time it takes for aluminum to break dowvn in a landfill: 80–100 years! Wonder what happens to the other things you throw away? Here's how long it takes for different materials to decompose in a landfill.

Recycling
1 ALUMINUM CAN
saves

95%

of the energy it would take to make a brand-new one.

GLASS BOTTLES: **1 MILLION YEARS**

STYROFOAM CUPS & PLASTIC BAGS: **UP TO FOREVER!**

COUNT YOUR PENNIES

The next time you find a cent on the ground, don't pass it by!
All those pennies in your piggy bank, sock drawer, and sofa cushions really add up. Just how many pennies are out there? Read on to find out!

OVER 200,000,000,000

1.67 CENTS
Amount of money it costs the U.S. Mint to make a penny.

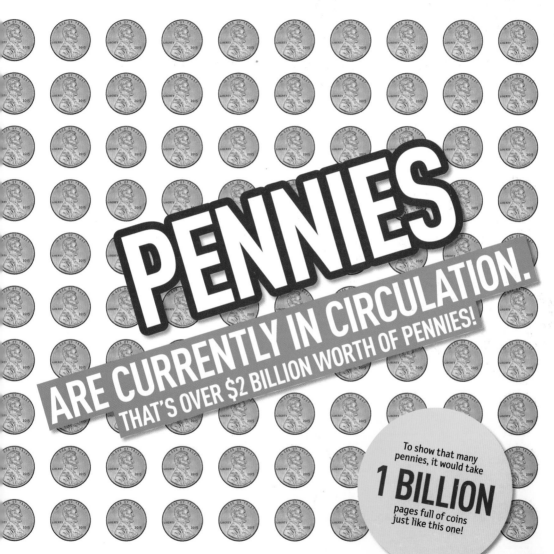

PENNIES

ARE CURRENTLY IN CIRCULATION.

THAT'S OVER $2 BILLION WORTH OF PENNIES!

To show that many
pennies, it would take

1 BILLION

pages full of coins
just like this one!

SNOWBOARDING WITH SHAUN

Shaun White started out as a skateboarder, but once he stepped onto a snowboard, he never looked back! Check out some of Shaun's sick achievements on the slopes.

Birthday:
SEPTEMBER 3, 1986

Age Shaun went pro in skateboarding:
13

Kids rule the slopes!
28.5%
of snowboarders are between the ages of 6 and 17.

Age Shaun started snowboarding:
6

Number of
Winter Olympics
competed in:

3

Number of twists
in Shaun's Double McTwist
trick:

3.5

That's a
1260° turn!

Snurf's up!
Snowboarding
was originally called
snurfing. That's "snow"
and "surfing" put
together!

Number of
Olympic medals:

2 GOLD

Number of X Games
medals:

**15 GOLD,
5 SILVER,
3 BRONZE**

CRUNCHING ON **CHIPS**

Craving a salty snack? Potato chips will do the trick! The average American eats over 4 pounds (1.8 kg) of potato chips every year. Here's how they're made.

STEP 1 EVERY CHIP STARTS AS A POTATO.

POTATOES ARE DELIVERED TO THE CHIP FACTORY. IT TAKES

100 POUNDS → 25 POUNDS

(45.4 KG) OF RAW POTATOES TO MAKE

(11.3 KG)

OF CHIPS.

STEP 2 THE POTATOES ARE WASHED, PEELED,

AND CUT INTO THIN SLICES THAT MEASURE

.066–.072 INCHES

(1.7–1.85 MM)

THICK.

STRAIGHT BLADES MAKE REGULAR CHIPS

AND RIPPLED BLADES MAKE RIDGED CHIPS.

STEP 3 THE SLICES ARE RINSED, DRIED, AND FRIED IN OIL THAT IS

350–375°F
(176.6–190.5°C)

STEP 4 SALT IS SPRINKLED ONTO THE CHIPS AT A RATE OF ABOUT

1.75 POUNDS
(0.79 KG)
OF SALT TO EVERY

100 POUNDS
(45.4 KG) OF CHIPS.

STEP 5 THE HOT CHIPS ARE COOLED, WEIGHED, AND PACKED INTO BAGS, READY FOR SNACKING!

DREAM JOB ALERT! Taste testers check chips from each batch about **1 TIME PER HOUR.**

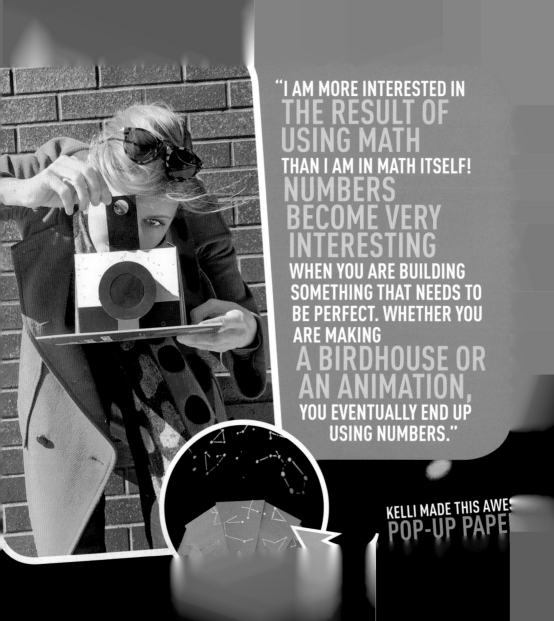

"I AM MORE INTERESTED IN **THE RESULT OF USING MATH** THAN I AM IN MATH ITSELF! **NUMBERS BECOME VERY INTERESTING** WHEN YOU ARE BUILDING SOMETHING THAT NEEDS TO BE PERFECT. WHETHER YOU ARE MAKING **A BIRDHOUSE OR AN ANIMATION,** YOU EVENTUALLY END UP USING NUMBERS."

KELLI MADE THIS AWE
POP-UP PAPE

AN INTERVIEW WITH KELLI ANDERSON

INFORMATION DESIGNER & ARTIST

Q: WHAT IS IT THAT YOU DO?

A: I use paper (plus design) to make interactive demonstrations of data. One of my recent projects is a pop-up paper planetarium. You can use it with your iPhone to project the night sky onto the ceiling. I've also made a paper record player and a paper camera.

Q: HOW DO PEOPLE BENEFIT FROM YOUR WORK?

A: My work helps people understand concepts that are otherwise difficult to observe. This allows people to reflect on themselves and how we all navigate this information-saturated modern life.

Q: ANY ADVICE FOR THE NEXT GENERATION OF DATA DESIGNERS?

A: If you have a question, see if you can test it out yourself first rather than going immediately to Google. This practice helps you develop strategies to think for yourself. When you think for yourself, you automatically have something new to offer the world!

GENTLE GIANTS

Roaming the grasslands of Africa, giraffes tower over every other animal. In fact, they're the world's tallest mammals! But just how tall are they? The answer might surprise you!

SIZE:
14—19 FEET (4–6 M)

NECK LENGTH:
6 FEET (1.8 M)

A GIRAFFE'S NECK ALONE WEIGHS ABOUT **600 POUNDS!** [272 KG]

TONGUE LENGTH:
21 [53 CM] **INCHES**

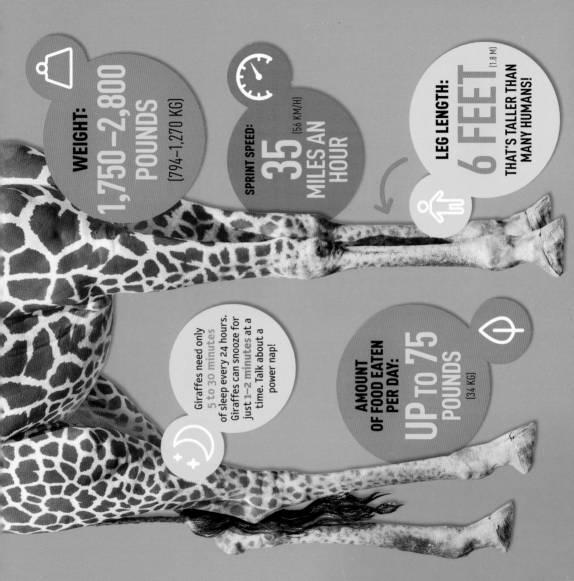

WEIGHT:
1,750–2,800 POUNDS
[794–1,270 KG]

SPRINT SPEED:
35 MILES AN HOUR
[56 KM/H]

LEG LENGTH:
6 FEET [1.8 M]
THAT'S TALLER THAN MANY HUMANS!

Giraffes need only 5 to 30 minutes of sleep every 24 hours. Giraffes can snooze for just 1–2 minutes at a time. Talk about a power nap!

AMOUNT OF FOOD EATEN PER DAY:
UP TO 75 POUNDS
[34 KG]

INTERNATIONAL PEDAL POWER

Want to go on a bike ride? With over 800 million bicycles on the road worldwide, they are one of the most popular ways to get around. Strap on your helmet and pedal your way around the 10 most bike-friendly cities in the world.

1. COPENHAGEN, DENMARK

63% OF PEOPLE IN COPENHAGEN BIKE TO SCHOOL OR WORK. ONLY **10%** DRIVE A CAR!

2. AMSTERDAM, NETHERLANDS

800,000 PEOPLE IN AMSTERDAM RIDE A BIKE EVERY DAY.

3. UTRECHT, NETHERLANDS

96% OF HOUSEHOLDS IN UTRECHT HAVE **1 OR MORE** BIKES.

4. STRASBOURG, FRANCE

348 MILES (560 KM) OF BIKE PATHS WIND THROUGH THE CITY.

88% 🚲
of American households have a car, but only half have a bike.

THE COLOR OF THE BOX BEHIND EACH NUMBER MATCHES THE COLOR OF ITS LOCATION TAG.

5. EINDHOVEN, NETHERLANDS

6. MALMÖ, SWEDEN

7. NANTES, FRANCE

8. BORDEAUX, FRANCE

9. ANTWERP, BELGIUM

10. SEVILLE, SPAIN

BRAIN-BOGGLING STATS

What's small enough to fit in your hands but can control your whole body? It's your brain! This 3-pound (1.4-kg) powerhouse can do some really incredible things, like helping us learn and moving our bodies. It even works when we're sleeping! Wrap your mind around these cool facts about what's happening inside your cranium.

70,000
Number of thoughts some scientists think your brain has each day

400 MILES (644 km)
Length of blood vessels inside the brain if you put them all together

24 HOURS
Number of hours a day your brain is working, whether you're awake or asleep

260 MILES AN HOUR (418 km/h)
Speed some brain signals can travel between neurons

100 BILLION
Number of neurons inside the brain

TURN UP THE TUNES

What's that song? Turn up the volume with this timeline of famous tunes that are sure to get stuck in your head!

1956
Elvis Presley
"Hound Dog"

1975
Queen
"Bohemian Rhapsody"

1950 **1955** **1960** **1965** **1970** **1975** **1980**

1965
The Rolling Stones
"I Can't Get No Satisfaction"

1963
The Beatles
"I Want to Hold Your Hand"

1980
Devo
"Whip It"

1992
Whitney Houston
"I Will Always Love You"

2014
Taylor Swift
"Shake It Off"

2003
Beyoncé
"Crazy in Love"

| 1985 | 1990 | 1995 | 2000 | 2005 | 2010 | 2015 |

1998
Britney Spears
"... Baby One More Time"

2010
Justin Bieber
"Baby"

AMAZING **ANACONDAS**

Slithering through the tropical rain forests of South America, green anacondas are the biggest snakes on Earth, both in length and weight. Just how big are they? Read on to find out!

LIFE SPAN:

10 YEARS

WEIGHT:

500 POUNDS
(227 KG)

THAT'S AS HEAVY AS
9 KIDS!

DIAMETER:

12 INCHES
(30.5 CM)

LENGTH:

30 FEET (9 M)

THAT'S AS LONG AS 7 TEN-YEAR-OLDS LYING DOWN HEAD TO FOOT!

These super-sized snakes have giant appetites to match, snacking on **wild pigs, deer, birds, turtles, and even jaguars.** After swallowing their dinner whole, they can go for weeks (or even months!) without food.

Do you play a sport? 56.6% of kids ages 6 to 12 in the U.S. play team sports. But what are they playing? Here's the percentage of girls and boys who play each sport.

25% BASKETBALL

17% BASEBALL/ SOFTBALL

17% SOCCER

GIRLS

17% TRACK

23% VOLLEYBALL

12% SWIMMING
8% TENNIS
4% CROSS COUNTRY
3% LACROSSE

40% FOOTBALL

20% SOCCER

BOYS

17% TRACK

24% BASEBALL

40% BASKETBALL

10% WRESTLING
9% SWIMMING
8% TENNIS
5% CROSS COUNTRY

GIRLS AND BOYS AGREE: BASKETBALL RULES! Basketball is the most popular sport played by both boys and girls in the U.S.

Time for bed! Babies need a lot of sleep. But how does their sleep compare to other baby animals? Tuck yourself in and enjoy these bedtime facts.

NEWBORN BABIES CAN SLEEP UP TO

18 HOURS A DAY.

THAT'S THE SAME AMOUNT OF TIME

A PUPPY SLEEPS!

Throughout the years, kids from all generations have had their favorite toys. Here's a look back at some of the biggest toy fads of the past 80 years.

1945
SLINKY

This magical walking spring was very popular in the **1950s**. Slinkys were originally priced at **$1**. In its first decade of sales, some **100 MILLION** Slinkys were sold.

1943
SILLY PUTTY

Silly Putty's recipe was discovered accidentally by a chemical engineer in **1943**, but the toy didn't become popular until it was featured in a **1950** issue of the *New Yorker*. Over **250,000** plastic eggs filled with Silly Putty were sold in **3 DAYS**.

1950
MAGIC 8 BALL

The original mechanism inside a Magic 8 Ball was invented as a fortune-telling device. There are **20** different answers printed on the **20-SIDED** die that floats inside a Magic 8 Ball: **10** are positive, **5** are negative, and **5** are neutral.

1959
BARBIE

Barbie is over **50 YEARS OLD**, but she's still one of the most popular toys of all time. Over a **BILLION** Barbies have been sold since her introduction in the late **1950s**.

1996
TICKLE ME ELMO

This talking stuffed Elmo doll sparked a toy craze when it unexpectedly sold out before Christmas. **1 MILLION** Elmos were sold during the **1996** holiday shopping season, with one person paying **$7,100** for one doll.

1977
RUBIK'S CUBE

Created by a Hungarian sculptor and architecture professor, the Rubik's Cube is a handheld puzzle made of colored squares. There are **43,252,003,274,489,856,000** different ways to arrange the original **3X3** Rubik's Cube.

2009
ANGRY BIRDS

This video game is the most popular free game of all time! As of **JULY 2015**, people have downloaded over **3 BILLION** Angry Birds games.

BLAST OFF!

Next stop: space! NASA created the Saturn V rocket to fly Apollo astronauts to the moon and back and to send the Skylab space station into orbit. Even though it was last flown in the 1970s, Saturn V is still the tallest, heaviest, and most powerful rocket ever launched. Here's a look at the massive size and power of this rocket.

HEIGHT:

365 FEET
[111 M]

THAT'S 57.5 FEET [17.5 M] **TALLER THAN THE STATUE OF LIBERTY!**

WEIGHT:

6.2 MILLION POUNDS
[2.8 MILLION KG]

THAT'S AS HEAVY AS 400 ELEPHANTS!

THRUST:

7.6 MILLION POUNDS
(34.5 MILLION NEWTONS)

THAT'S MORE ENERGY THAN 85 HOOVER DAMS!

WEIGHT IT CAN LAUNCH INTO ORBIT:

130 TONS
(118,000 KG)

THAT'S MORE THAN 10 SCHOOL BUSES!

800 TIMES

A car that gets 30 miles (48 km) per gallon could drive around Earth 800 TIMES with the amount of fuel that Saturn V used to fly to the moon. That's one giant gas tank!

BEAR SMACKDOWN

The forests and mountains of the United States are home to 2 kinds of bears: black bears and grizzly bears. They may look similar, but what makes them different? It's a battle of the bears!

BLACK BEAR

WEIGHT: **200–600 POUNDS** (91–272 KG)

CLAW

LENGTH: (3.8 CM) **1.5 INCHES**

Black bears live in a home range of **15–80 SQUARE MILES** (39–207 SQ KM)

30 FASTEST SPEED: (48 KM/H) **MILES AN HOUR**

AVERAGE LIFE SPAN: **20 YEARS**

TOTAL BODY LENGTH: (1.5–1.8 M) **5–6 FEET**

GRIZZLY BEAR

WEIGHT:
800 POUNDS [363 KG]

CLAW LENGTH:
2–4 INCHES [5–10 CM]

FASTEST SPEED:
30 MILES AN HOUR [48 KM/H]

AVERAGE LIFE SPAN:
25 YEARS

TOTAL BODY LENGTH:
5–8 FEET [1.5–2.5 M]

Grizzlies are the **2ND LARGEST BEAR** in North America, after the polar bear.

HEARTBEATS

Your heart works hard to pump blood through your body, beating 24 hours a day, 7 days a week, 365 days a year. How does your heart rate compare to an animal's average heartbeat? Let's find out!

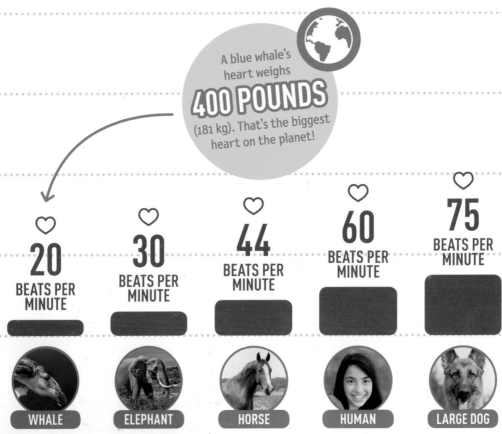

A blue whale's heart weighs **400 POUNDS** (181 kg). That's the biggest heart on the planet!

20 BEATS PER MINUTE — WHALE

30 BEATS PER MINUTE — ELEPHANT

44 BEATS PER MINUTE — HORSE

60 BEATS PER MINUTE — HUMAN

75 BEATS PER MINUTE — LARGE DOG

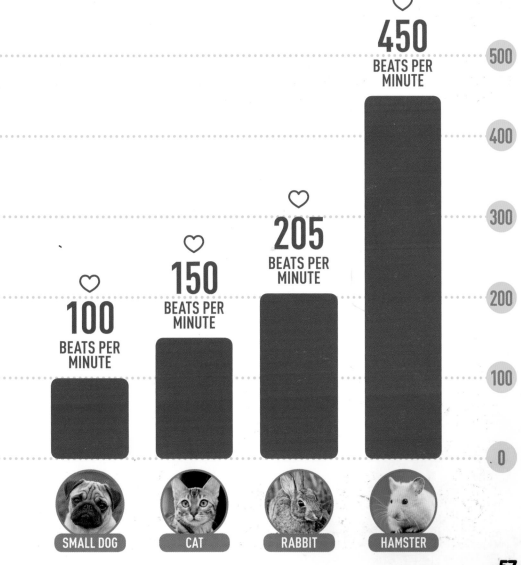

♡ 450 BEATS PER MINUTE

♡ 205 BEATS PER MINUTE

♡ 150 BEATS PER MINUTE

♡ 100 BEATS PER MINUTE

500
400
300
200
100
0

SMALL DOG

CAT

RABBIT

HAMSTER

PI CHART

Pi—or the ratio of a circle's circumference to its diameter—has mystified mathematicians for centuries. Since it's a special number that goes on forever, our knowledge of pi is limited by the technology we have to count its digits. How many numbers have we crunched to date? Read on to find out!

3.14159265358979323846264338
9445923078164062
8086513282306647
4811174502841027
19644288810975665
0190914564856692
0249141273724587
5409171536436789

27950288419716939937510582097

5208998628034825342117067982 14

9384460955058223172535940812 8

9385211055596446229489549303 8

3446128475648233786783165271 2

6034861045432664821339360726

6606315588174881520920962829 2

9036001133053054882046652 13 ...

HIGH **HOPPERS**

There are nearly 45 different species of kangaroos and wallabies hopping through the forests and grasslands of Australia and Tasmania. Powerful hind legs help these marsupials run and bound at amazing speeds and distances! Jump in and check out these rockin' 'roo facts.

JUMP LENGTH:

25 FEET

(7.6 M) IN A SINGLE LEAP

JUMP HEIGHT:

6 FEET (1.8 M)

THAT'S TALLER THAN MOST ADULTS!

LONG DISTANCE SPEED:

15
MILES AN HOUR
(24 KM/H)

SPRINT SPEED:

OVER 35
MILES AN HOUR
(56 KM/H)

THAT'S FASTER THAN USAIN BOLT, THE FASTEST RUNNER IN THE WORLD! HIS TOP SPRINT SPEED IS 28 MILES AN HOUR (45 KM/H).

Newborn baby kangaroos— called joeys—are just **1 INCH** (2.5 cm) long. That's about the size of a grape!

61

VIDEO GAME HEROES

Today, you can carry a video game in your pocket. But in the 1970s, people played on giant game machines that were taller than you! From old-school arcades to new mobile games, let's travel through video game history and learn how our favorite pixilated protagonists got their start.

1978 SPACE INVADERS
Japanese company Taito releases Space Invaders, kicking off the golden age of video arcade games. In **1 YEAR**, the company installed over **100,000** Space Invaders machines. It became so popular that entire arcades were filled with just this one game!

1981 DONKEY KONG
Nintendo makes Donkey Kong, the first arcade game to feature jumping, multiple stages, and a playable story. Because of an error in the game's code, you can't play past the **22ND LEVEL**.

1975   1980   1985   1990

1980
PAC-MAN
This iconic yellow character has been chomping ghosts for over **30 YEARS!** In **2013**, game player David Race set the world record for achieving the maximum Pac-Man score of **3,333,360 POINTS** in just **3 HOURS, 28 MINUTES, AND 49 SECONDS**.

1983
MARIO
Mario and his brother, Luigi, are the most popular plumbers on the planet! Nintendo's Shigeru Miyamoto and a team of **7 ARTISTS** and programmers created the first Mario game. Since then, the Mario brothers have been featured in over **220 DIFFERENT VIDEO GAMES!**

1996

PIKACHU

This electric monster is from the best-selling role-playing video game of all time! Starting with just **2 GAMES** and **151 POKEMON**, the universe has grown to include nearly **30 GAMES** and **721 DIFFERENT CATCHABLE CREATURES.**

2009

RED

This angry avian is the main hero in the battle against pigs! Red can be found in the Angry Birds series of games, TV shows, movies, and more. Angry Birds has been downloaded over **3 BILLION TIMES,** making it the most downloaded free phone game ever.

1995   2000   2005   2010

1986

SAMUS

Star of the Metroid games, Samus Aran is not only a fierce fighter. She is also the first playable human female character in a mainstream video game. The entire Metroid series has sold over **17.44 MILLION COPIES** since it debuted.

2007

CHELL

Darting through wormholes in the game Portal, players solve puzzles as heroine Chell. The popular game has been downloaded over **1.5 MILLION TIMES.**

Checkmate! A friendly game of chess is fun, but did you know there's lots of math at play, too? Make your move with these unbelievable chess facts.

THERE ARE OVER

318 BILLION

DIFFERENT WAYS

In **1988,** a computer called Deep Thought became the first machine to beat an international grandmaster chess player.

The first game of chess played between a person on Earth and an astronaut in space was on **JUNE 9, 1970.** The game ended in a draw.

TO PLAY THE FIRST 4 MOVES ON BOTH SIDES IN A CHESS GAME.

The longest tournament chess game between two people lasted for **269 MOVES.**

Kirk and Spock played chess on the original Star Trek show **3 TIMES.** Guess who won all **3 GAMES?** Kirk!

FAVORITE FOOD FACTS

What's on your dinner plate? Researchers surveyed over 1,400 kids from ages 8 to 18 and asked them to rate the foods they love to eat. Which delicious dish tops the menu? Read on to find out!

#8
Mashed potatoes

#10
Hamburger

#9
Strawberries

#6
Tacos

#5
Chicken nuggets

#7
Doughnuts

Least favorite food:
BLACK-EYED PEAS!

45%
of kids surveyed said they would never eat them!

#4
Tater tots

#3
Chocolate milk

#1
Pizza

#2
French fries

NOW THAT'S A **BIG RIG!**

If you've ever been on a road trip, chances are high you've seen these giant 18-wheelers barreling down the road. So how big are they? Buckle up and find out!

SEMITRAILERS ARE **53 FEET LONG.**

(16.1 M)

THAT'S AS LONG AS
3 ASIAN ELEPHANTS!

Semitrucks drive about **140 BILLION MILES** (225 billion km) a year in the U.S. That's like driving around the Earth **5.6 MILLION** times!

If you've seen an owl in your backyard at night, it could have been this one! The great horned owl is the most common owl in the Americas. Learn more about these feathered friends.

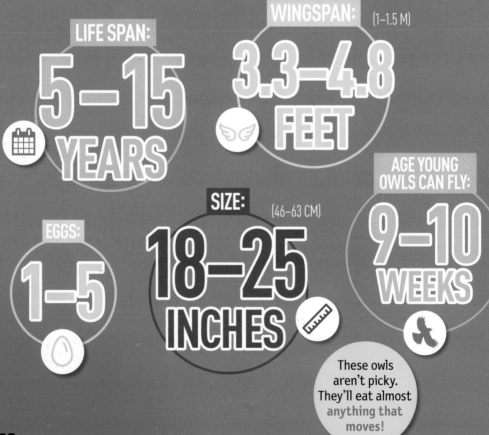

LIFE SPAN:
5—15 YEARS

WINGSPAN: (1–1.5 M)
3.3—4.8 FEET

AGE YOUNG OWLS CAN FLY:
9—10 WEEKS

EGGS:
1-5

SIZE: (46–63 CM)
18—25 INCHES

These owls aren't picky. They'll eat almost anything that moves!

Despite its name, this owl doesn't actually have horns! The "horns" are really **tufts of feathers** on top of the owl's head.

WEIGHT: (1–2.5 KG)

2–5.5 POUNDS

NEST HEIGHT:

20–60 FEET ABOVE GROUND
(6–18 M)

INCUBATION:

28–35 DAYS

INCREDIBLE INVENTORS

From the lightbulb to movie cameras, Thomas Edison holds over 1,000 patents for his inventions. But young inventors are making history, too! Explore this gallery of kid-made inventions.

POPSICLE

In **1905**, **11-YEAR-OLD** Frank Epperson left his soda outside overnight. When it froze inside the cup with a stirring stick inside, the Popsicle was born! There are now **26 DIFFERENT FLAVORS** of Popsicle-brand treats.

AGE OF INVENTOR:

11

AGE OF INVENTOR:

15

TELEVISION

Can you believe a kid invented the TV? **15-YEAR-OLD** Philo Farnsworth was sitting in high school chemistry class when he sketched out a system to electronically transmit images. His discoveries are still used in electronics today.

BRAILLE

Louis Braille was just 3 YEARS OLD when he became blind. At 16 YEARS OLD, he started poking holes in paper to represent letters. By 1824, he had invented Braille, the reading system that is used by blind people around the world.

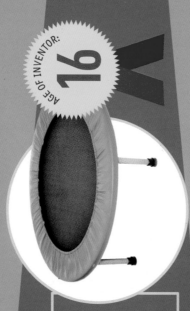

AGE OF INVENTOR: 16

AGE OF INVENTOR: 16

TRAMPOLINE

16-YEAR-OLD diver and gymnast George Nissen invented the trampoline in 1930. He first came up with the idea for his new gymnastic apparatus after watching trapeze artists fall into the net. Trampoline became a short-lived Olympic sport in 2000.

ECO-FRIENDLY EXHAUST

17-YEAR-OLD Param Jaggi wants to clean up the atmosphere! This young scientist invented a box that attaches to a car's tailpipe and uses algae to turn exhaust emissions into oxygen. The cost? Just $30!

AGE OF INVENTOR: 17

FAST-FOOD HABITS

When was the last time you pulled into the drive-through for a quick bite? Check out how often the average American eats at a fast-food restaurant.

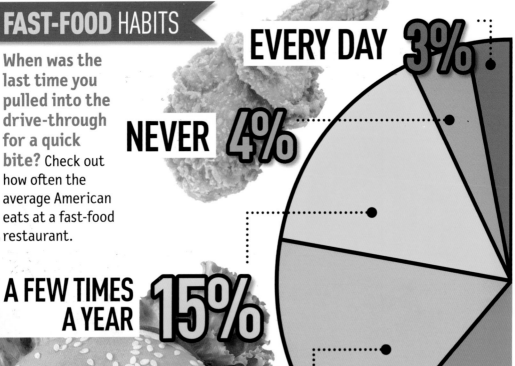

EVERY DAY 3%

NEVER 4%

A FEW TIMES A YEAR 15%

SEVERAL TIMES A WEEK 16%

33% ONCE OR TWICE A MONTH

28% ABOUT ONCE A WEEK

8 IN 10
Americans eat fast food at least **1 TIME** a month.

Nearly **50%** of Americans eat fast food at least **1 TIME** a week.

SCOTT'S YEAR IN **SPACE**

In 2016, Scott Kelly became the first American astronaut to complete a nearly yearlong mission in space. Living on the International Space Station with a Russian astronaut, Scott gave scientists a chance to study what happens when the human body stays in space for a long time. His research will help other astronauts prepare for future missions to Mars and beyond. Here's a look at the numbers behind Scott's record-breaking mission.

ALMOST 400

Number of different scientific studies Scott completed during his year in space, including growing the first flowering plant to ever bloom in space

4

Number of times Scott has been in space

340

Number of consecutive days Scott spent in space

520

Number of total days Scott has spent in space. That's more than any other American!

1 YEAR

The amount of time it took Scott to train and prepare for his year in space

3 Number of spacewalks Scott did during his year in space

THE WIDE WORLD OF SPORTS

All around the world, sports players and fans alike love to come together and enjoy a good game. Take a trip around the world and visit some of the biggest landmarks in sports.

RIO DE JANEIRO, BRAZIL

173,850

Number of people who watched Brazil play against Uruguay during the **1950 World Cup**. Maracanã Stadium was the site of the most attended soccer match in history.

DAYTONA BEACH, FLORIDA

500 MILES (805 km)

Length of the famous **Daytona 500** motor race. Held every year since **1959**, drivers make **200 laps** around the 2.5-mile (4-km)-long track and complete **4 turns** per lap.

JOHANNESBURG, SOUTH AFRICA

94,736

Number of soccer fans that can fit in FNB Stadium, the biggest sports stadium in Africa.

WIMBLEDON, LONDON
11 HOURS, 5 MINUTES

Length of a tennis match at the **2010** Wimbledon Championships. It took **3 days.** That's the longest tennis match on record!

FRANCE
2,200 MILES (3,500 km)

Distance of cycling's most famous race, the Tour de France. The race lasts for **23 days** and leads riders through the mountains of France and into the city of Paris.

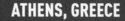

ATHENS, GREECE
241

Number of athletes who participated in the first modern Olympic Games in **1896.** They were from **14 countries** and participated in **43 events** across **9 different sports.**

EGG SIZE COMPARISONS

Different size birds lay different size eggs.
Let's visualize how big they are by comparing them to some common foods.

HUMMINGBIRD EGG = PEA OR JELLY BEAN

CROW EGG = APRICOT

GREAT HORNED OWL EGG = TANGERINE

AMERICAN ROBIN EGG = GRAPE

CANADA GOOSE EGG
= AVOCADO

The largest bird egg ever was laid by the now-extinct elephant bird that lived on Madagascar. Its giant

12-INCH

(31-cm) fossilized egg was discovered by archaeologists in the late 1800s or early 1900s.

OSTRICH EGG
= GRAPEFRUIT

HUGE **HAILSTONE**

Have you ever seen ice fall from the sky? During some thunderstorms, water droplets can be blown upward at speeds up to 110 miles an hour (180 km/h). Once the droplets reach colder air, they can freeze into pieces of ice that fall along with the raindrops. Most hailstones measure 0.2–1.75 inches (0.5–4.4 cm), but sometimes they grow as more water freezes to the hail. How big can they get? Read on to find out!

THE LARGEST HAILSTONE
ON RECORD MEASURED

This record-setting hailstone fell in Vivian, South Dakota, U.S.A., on
JULY 23, 2010.

8 INCHES

(20.3 CM)

IN DIAMETER.

THAT'S ALMOST AS BIG AS A

SOCCER BALL!

 These falling balls of ice can be expensive. Hail causes about **$1 BILLION OF DAMAGE** to property and crops each year in the U.S.

 Large hail usually comes from rotating thunderstorms called supercells. If you see hail, watch out— **ABOUT 30% OF THESE STORMS CAUSE TORNADOES.**

AN INTERVIEW WITH DATA RESEARCHER JON SCHWABISH

"BE INTERESTED IN LOTS OF DIFFERENT THINGS! WORKING WITH DATA REQUIRES NOT ONLY A STRONG FOUNDATION IN MATH, BUT ALSO WRITING, SPEAKING, AND THINKING VISUALLY. LOOK AROUND AT ART, DESIGN, AND SCIENCE TO FIND INSPIRATION!"

Q: WHAT DO YOU DO?

A: I have my own company that helps people and organizations improve the ways they use and communicate their data. I also work with a nonprofit research institution in Washington, D.C., to understand how government does (or doesn't) help people who need it.

Q: HOW DID YOU FIRST GET INTERESTED IN MATH AND NUMBERS?

A: When I was a kid, I was really into baseball. I collected tons of baseball cards, and I would scan the box scores in the newspaper every day. I became interested in how a batting average was calculated and looking at the player rankings and team standings. When I was in high school, I loved algebra and calculus. (I know, you don't hear many people say that, do you?) Then, later on, I went to college and then graduate school, to take math and apply it to data so that I could understand how the world works.

Q: WHAT IS IT ABOUT NUMBERS AND DATA THAT FASCINATES YOU?

A: I think what's great about numbers and data is that we can use them to better understand the world around us, and then try to improve our world. We need data, for example, to understand how our climate is changing. We can gather data on frequency of storms and global temperatures. We can then use those numbers and data to determine things we can do to help slow climate change or prepare for changes ahead. Without numbers and data—and without math to understand what they are telling us—we can't understand the problems, never mind develop solutions.

HOLIDAY HOOPLA

Every day is a party when you celebrate these wacky holidays!

Sure, they might not be the most popular holidays, but why let that stop you? Get out your calendar and save these special dates for a party of your own!

FIRST FRIDAY IN JUNE

NATIONAL DOUGHNUT DAY

No wonder doughnuts have their own day: More than 10 BILLION doughnuts are made (and eaten!) in America every year! This holiday has been celebrated in the U.S. since 1938.

LAST MONDAY IN JANUARY

BUBBLE WRAP APPRECIATION DAY

Get your popping fingers ready! If you love the snapping sound of bubble wrap, you're not alone. People have been popping bubble wrap since it was invented in 1957!

SEPTEMBER 19

TALK LIKE A PIRATE DAY

Shiver me timbers! Celebrated across the seven seas since 2002, this day is *arrr*-guably the most fun holiday ever. Put on an eye patch, grab your sword, and tell all your mateys "Ahoy!"

AUGUST 26

NATIONAL DOG DAY

Pamper your favorite pup on National Dog Day! First started in 2004, this holiday honors the around 80 MILLION dogs living in America. 37–47% of American families have a dog!

THIRD SATURDAY IN OCTOBER

SWEETEST DAY

Created in the 1920s by a candy company worker in Cleveland, Ohio, U.S.A., it's like Valentine's Day in October. Another excuse to enjoy some chocolate? Bring it on!

HOW MANY MOONS?

Look up in the night sky and you'll see our moon. But did you know that astronomers have discovered at least 182 moons orbiting planets in our solar system? Get to know them with this moon map.

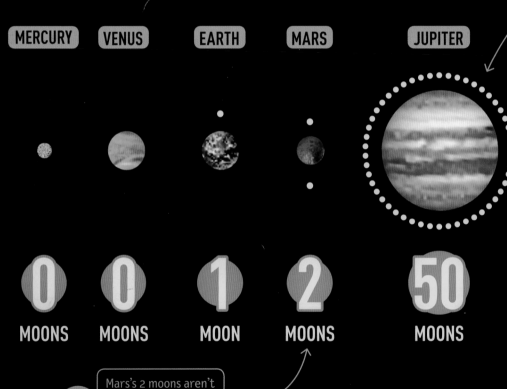

MERCURY

VENUS

EARTH

MARS

JUPITER

0 MOONS

0 MOONS

1 MOON

2 MOONS

50 MOONS

Mars's 2 moons aren't round and bright like ours. Instead, they are **lumpy** and **dark**.

Jupiter's moon Ganymede is the **largest moon** in the solar system.

SATURN

URANUS

NEPTUNE

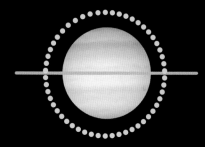

53
MOONS

27
MOONS

14
MOONS

Europa, another one of Jupiter's moons, is thought to have a deep saltwater ocean beneath its icy shell.

Get ready for a supercharged ride! Kingda Ka at Six Flags Great Adventure in New Jersey is not only the world's tallest roller coaster—it's the world's second fastest, too! Hang on tight and check out these adrenaline-pumping facts.

HEIGHT:

456 FEET
(139 M)

THAT'S AS TALL AS A 45-STORY BUILDING!

DROP:

418 FEET
(127 M)

129-FOOT-TALL
(39-M)
CAMEL HUMP

CLIMB ANGLE

90°

RIDE DURATION:

50.6

SECONDS

SPEED:

128

MILES PER HOUR

(206 KM/H)

HAVE A NEED FOR SPEED? RIDERS REACH TOP SPEED IN JUST 3.5 SECONDS!

LENGTH:

3,118 FEET

(950 M)

How common is your name? Explore this list of the most popular first names for babies born in the United States between 1916 and 2015.

6. David

15. Donald

9. Thomas

13. Betty

4. Elizabeth

18. Steven

7. Susan

1. James

11. Christopher

11. Karen

2. Patricia

3. Robert

13. Matthew

16. Sandra

12. Nancy

17. Ashley

8. Jessica

7. Richard

10. Sarah
14. Dorothy
10. Charles
12. Daniel
5. William
15. Lisa
17. Paul
3. Jennifer
6. Barbara
18. Kimberly
2. John
19. George
20. Kenneth
19. Donna
8. Joseph
16. Mark
5. Linda
1. Mary
4. Michael
20. Carol
9. Margaret
14. Anthony

During these 100 years, **172 MILLION BOYS** and **168 MILLION GIRLS** were born in the U.S.A.!

SODA POP SAYINGS

Want a pop? How about a soda? Or maybe a Coke? Depending on where you live, you might use a different word for these fizzy drinks. Check out this chart and see which name rules in your neck of the woods.

WHICH TERM IS MOST POPULAR ACROSS THE WHOLE U.S.?

41% SODA

ALASKA
ARIZONA
CALIFORNIA
CONNECTICUT
FLORIDA
HAWAII
MAINE
MARYLAND
MASSACHUSETTS
MISSOURI
NEVADA
NEW HAMPSHIRE
NEW JERSEY
NEW YORK
NORTH CAROLINA
RHODE ISLAND
UTAH
VERMONT
VIRGINIA
WISCONSIN

The average American drinks almost **45 GALLONS** (170 L) of carbonated soft drinks each year. That's enough soda to fill a bathtub!

What else do you call it? **"Soft drink"** and **"soda pop"** top the list of "other" options!

15% COKE

39% POP

5% OTHER

COLORADO
DELAWARE
IDAHO
ILLINOIS
INDIANA
IOWA
KANSAS
MICHIGAN
MINNESOTA
MONTANA
NEBRASKA
NORTH DAKOTA
OHIO
OKLAHOMA
OREGON
PENNSYLVANIA
SOUTH DAKOTA
WASHINGTON
WEST VIRGINIA
WYOMING

ALABAMA
ARKANSAS
GEORGIA
KENTUCKY
LOUISIANA

MISSISSIPPI
NEW MEXICO
SOUTH CAROLINA
TENNESSEE
TEXAS

CELESTIAL COUNTS

Have you ever wondered what's floating around out there in space?
Our solar system is made up of the sun and all of the objects that orbit around it. Read on to meet the planets, asteroids, and comets that make up our galactic neighborhood.

715,000+ ASTEROIDS

8 PLANETS
Mercury, Venus, Earth, Mars, Jupiter, Saturn, Uranus, Neptune

147 MOONS

300+ space exploration missions

5
DWARF PLANETS

Ceres, Makemake, Haumea, Eris, Pluto. And those are just the ones we've discovered. There could be many more!

1
STAR
(That's the sun!)

Only **0.2%** of the solar system's mass is made up of the 8 planets. The other **99.8%** is the sun!

3,400+
COMETS

9 BILLION
MILES
(15 BILLION KM)

from the sun to the edge of the solar system

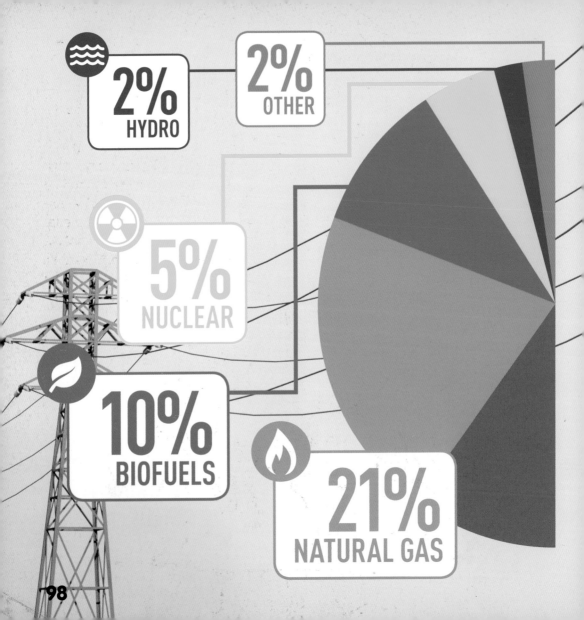

2% HYDRO

2% OTHER

5% NUCLEAR

10% BIOFUELS

21% NATURAL GAS

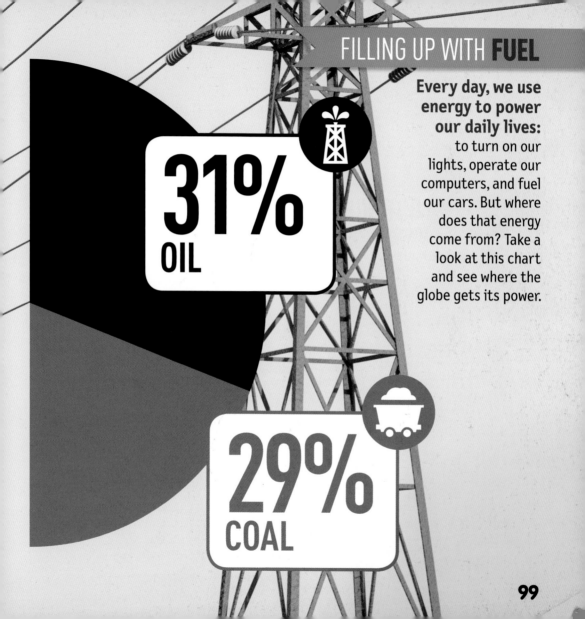

31%
OIL

29%
COAL

Every day, we use energy to power our daily lives: to turn on our lights, operate our computers, and fuel our cars. But where does that energy come from? Take a look at this chart and see where the globe gets its power.

NO-FLY ZONE

These birds may have wings, but you won't see them in the air anytime soon. Instead of flying, these unique birds have found other creative ways to get around. Check them out below!

OSTRICH

The ostrich is the largest bird on Earth, measuring up to

9 FEET TALL
(2.7 m) and weighing up to

300 POUNDS.
(136 kg)

These big birds can't fly, but they can run up to

45 MILES AN HOUR!
(72.4 km/h)

PENGUIN

Penguins can't fly through the sky, but they can whiz through the water at speeds of up to

15
MILES AN HOUR!
(25 km/h)

They use their short legs to waddle across the ice and dive into the water as deep as

1,850 FEET
(565 m)

All
5 SPECIES
of kiwi birds living in New Zealand are wingless and can't fly.

But what they lack in wings they make up in eggs: These chicken-size kiwis lay eggs up to

1 POUND
(.45 kg) in weight, the biggest egg of any living species relative to the size of the bird.

NO FLY ZONE

KIWI

A PROPORTIONAL **WORLD**

Wonder why this map looks so weird?

A normal map shows how much land area each country has. But on this map, each country is scaled to show how many people live there. Explore this wacky map and discover some surprising facts about where people live!

Rate at Which the Number of People is Changing

- ■ Very fast increase
- ■ Fast increase
- ■ Medium increase
- ■ Slow increase
- ■ Decrease

Each square represents one million people.

NORTH AMERICA

EUROPE

AFRICA

SOUTH AMERICA

40 COUNTRIES have fewer than **1 MILLION PEOPLE** and aren't shown on this map: Andorra, Antigua and Barbuda, Bahamas, Barbados, Belize, Brunei, Cape Verde, Comoros, Cyprus, Djibouti, Dominica, Equatorial Guinea, Fiji, Grenada, Guyana, Iceland, Kiribati, Liechtenstein, Luxembourg,

China is home
to more than
1.3 BILLION
people, making it the world's
most populous country.

A S I A

AUSTRALIA

Maldives, Malta, Marshall Islands, Micronesia, Monaco, Nauru, Palau, Qatar, St. Kitts & Nevis,
St. Lucia, St. Vincent & The Grenadines, Samoa, San Marino, Sao Tome and Principe, Seychelles,
Solomon Islands, Suriname, Tonga, Tuvalu, Vanuatu, Vatican City

SURFING THE **SPECTRUM**

What do rainbows, microwaves, and television have in common?
They all exist thanks to electromagnetic energy! Okay, that may sound like sci-fi, but did you know electromagnetic energy is a huge part of our everyday lives? It can take many different forms, from the colors of light we know and love to invisible energy like radio waves and x-rays. Here's a look at the wave-filled world of the electromagnetic spectrum.

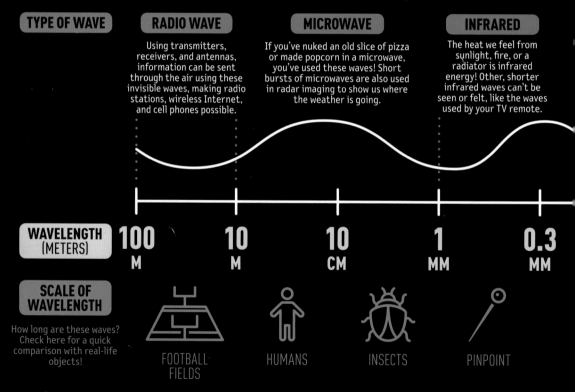

TYPE OF WAVE

RADIO WAVE
Using transmitters, receivers, and antennas, information can be sent through the air using these invisible waves, making radio stations, wireless Internet, and cell phones possible.

MICROWAVE
If you've nuked an old slice of pizza or made popcorn in a microwave, you've used these waves! Short bursts of microwaves are also used in radar imaging to show us where the weather is going.

INFRARED
The heat we feel from sunlight, fire, or a radiator is infrared energy! Other, shorter infrared waves can't be seen or felt, like the waves used by your TV remote.

WAVELENGTH (METERS)

100 M	10 M	10 CM	1 MM	0.3 MM

SCALE OF WAVELENGTH
How long are these waves? Check here for a quick comparison with real-life objects!

FOOTBALL FIELDS

HUMANS

INSECTS

PINPOINT

VISIBLE LIGHT

All the colors you see around you are part of the electromagnetic spectrum! These tiny visible light waves bounce off of objects and are picked up by the cones in our eyes. Each color is a different wavelength of light. Red has the longest wavelength (620–750 nanometers) and violet has the shortest (380–450 nm).

All of these waves travel at the speed of light, or about

186,282

MILES A SECOND

(299,792 KM/S).

ULTRAVIOLET

If you've ever gotten a sunburn, you've experienced ultraviolet light! These waves are invisible to humans, but some insects can see them!

X-RAY

These amazing rays can travel through skin and allow us to see inside the human body! Doctors can use x-rays to take pictures of your bones and teeth.

GAMMA RAY

Gamma rays might be small, but they pack the most energy of any wave in the entire electromagnetic spectrum. They're produced by the hottest parts of the universe and are the most powerful type of light energy.

780 NM   **380 NM**   **10 NM**   **0.01 NM**   **0.000001 NM**

PROTOZOA

MOLECULES

ATOMS

ATOMIC NUCLEI

SUBATOMIC PARTICLES

GREAT GOURDS

Fall is here! That means it's time for cooler weather, Halloween, and pumpkins, of course. Here are some fun facts about these bright orange fruits. (That's right—pumpkins aren't vegetables!)

A farmer once grew a pumpkin that weighed

2,323 POUNDS

(1,054 kg). That's as heavy as a rhinoceros!

Humans have been growing pumpkins for

10,000 YEARS.

Pumpkins take

85–120

days to grow, depending on the variety.

Farmers in the United States grow more than

1.9 BILLION
POUNDS

(862 million kg) of pumpkins every year.

Americans eat

50 MILLION

pumpkin pies every Thanksgiving!

If you eat 1 cup (225 g) of mashed pumpkin, you'll get

245%

of your recommended daily amount of vitamin A!

If you like sports, you probably love the Olympics! First started in 776 B.C., the ancient Olympics were held every 4 years until A.D. 393, when a Roman emperor canceled the games. It wasn't until 1896 that the tradition was revived by the International Olympic Committee, and it's been going strong ever since. Which country has won the most medals? Step onto the winner's stand and find out!

Gold medals aren't all gold! The last 100% gold medal was awarded in 1912. At the 2016 Rio Olympics, gold medals contained 0.2 OUNCE (6 G) of gold.

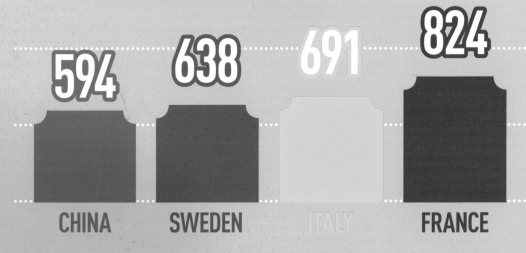

594	638	691	824
CHINA	SWEDEN	ITALY	FRANCE

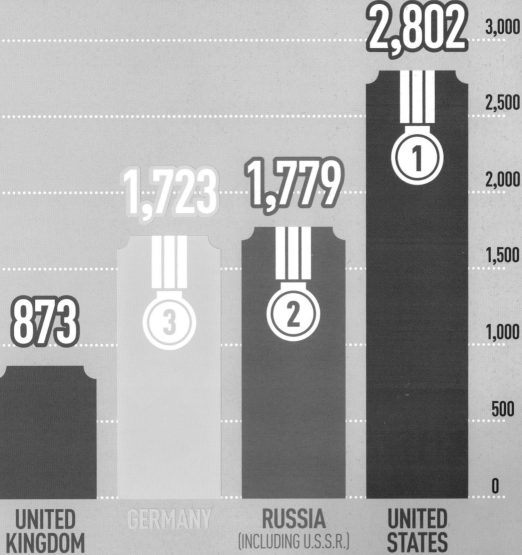

873
**UNITED
KINGDOM**

1,723
GERMANY

1,779
RUSSIA
(INCLUDING U.S.S.R.)

2,802
**UNITED
STATES**

3,000

2,500

2,000

1,500

1,000

500

0

What's your favorite book? 51% of kids in the U.S. are reading a book for fun. Find out what kids look for when picking their next page turner.

 70%
MAKES ME LAUGH

30%
IS A
LITTLE SCARY

 **17%**
HAS CHARACTERS
WHO ARE IN LOVE

54%
LETS ME USE MY
IMAGINATION

43%
TEACHES ME
SOMETHING NEW

41%
HAS A MYSTERY OR
PROBLEM TO SOLVE

Kids **AGES 6–11**
who read books for
fun **5–7 DAYS A WEEK**
read an average of

43.4
BOOKS PER YEAR.

LIFE IN THE SLOW LANE

Slow down and say hello to the slowest mammals on Earth! Spending nearly all of their lives in the treetops of Central and South America, three-toed sloths move so gradually that they often look like they aren't moving at all! Here are some surprising stats about these slow-motion mammals.

15–20 HOURS

Amount of time a day sloths spend asleep

8–9

Number of vertebrae in a sloth's neck, giving them extra flexibility. Most mammals have 7!

270°

Degrees a sloth can turn its head. That's almost all the way around!

Sloths are clumsy on land, but they're surprisingly good SWIMMERS!

HUNDREDS
Number of moths, beetles, cockroaches, and worms living in some sloths' fur

UP TO 30%
Percentage of body weight that can be taken up by food in a sloth's stomach after a big meal

4
Number of chambers in a sloth's stomach

PERIODIC TIMELINE OF THE **ELEMENTS**

The elements make up all of the matter in our universe, but when was each one discovered? Check out this elemental timeline and find out!

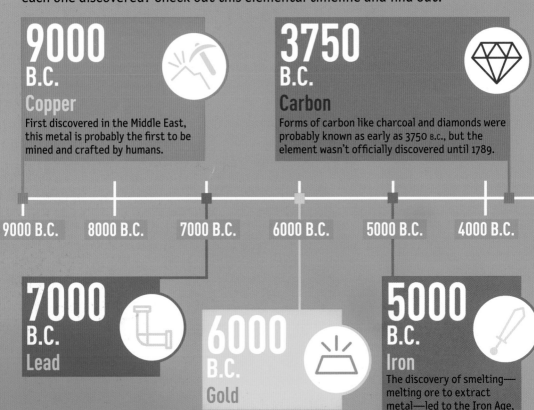

9000 B.C.
Copper
First discovered in the Middle East, this metal is probably the first to be mined and crafted by humans.

3750 B.C.
Carbon
Forms of carbon like charcoal and diamonds were probably known as early as 3750 B.C., but the element wasn't officially discovered until 1789.

9000 B.C. 8000 B.C. 7000 B.C. 6000 B.C. 5000 B.C. 4000 B.C.

7000 B.C.
Lead

6000 B.C.
Gold

5000 B.C.
Iron
The discovery of smelting—melting ore to extract metal—led to the Iron Age, in which people used iron to make tools and weapons.

In **1869**, D. I. Mendeleev organized the **64 ELEMENTS** known at that time into the first periodic table!

1772
Nitrogen
This colorless, odorless gas makes up about 80% of Earth's atmosphere—and the air we breathe!

2010
Tennessine
The most recently discovered element!

?

1766
Hydrogen

2000 B.C. | 1000 B.C. | 0 | 1000 | 2000 | 3000

1500 B.C.
Mercury
This liquid metal conducts electricity and used to be found in thermometers, although it's being replaced by new, safer technology.

20 B.C.
Zinc
You might find this metal is in your vitamins! Zinc is an essential trace element that is found in our red blood cells.

1771
Oxygen

1940
Neptunium
This element was first discovered in a lab. It is highly unstable and quickly decays into other elements.

A MALE RUBY-THROATED HUMMINGBIRD CAN WEIGH UP TO

.21 OUNCE.

(6 g)

A hummingbird's cranberry-size heart can beat up to

1,260

BEATS PER MINUTE.

Recently discovered fossils show that hummingbirds have been around for more than

30 MILLION YEARS.

What's that flash flying through your garden? Look fast, it's a hummingbird! All around the world, over 330 different species of hummingbirds flit from flower to flower, gathering nectar and doing daring tricks along the way. Say hello to the hummingbird!

THAT'S THE SAME AS

6 PAPER CLIPS!

REAL-LIFE SIZE!

An adult hummingbird may eat **2 TIMES** its body weight in food every day. That would be the equivalent of a 10-year-old eating about **560 HAMBURGERS** every day!

Hummingbirds can beat their wings up to **80 TIMES PER SECOND.**

A VERY QUICK TRIP

Want to go to the moon for the weekend? How about Mars?
Travel at the speed of light and you can get anywhere in a flash! Check out how long it would take you to tour the universe at light speed.

SPEED OF LIGHT:

186,282
MILES PER SECOND
(299,792 km/s)

VENUS:
2
MINUTES

MOON:
1.5
SECONDS

MARS:
4
MINUTES

Ready to see the edge of the observable universe?
Travel at light speed and you'll get there in
13.8 BILLION YEARS.
Good luck taking that much time off from school!

JUPITER:
30
MINUTES

NEPTUNE:
4
HOURS

SATURN:
1
HOUR

PLUTO:
5.5
HOURS

AMAZING **MAIZE**

In 2015, American farmers planted 88 million acres (35.6 million ha) of corn. That's a lot of ears! But they don't all end up on the dinner table—although the average American family does eat 25 pounds (11.3 kg) of corn a year. Discover the many other uses of corn below!

4% HIGH-FRUCTOSE CORN SYRUP

13% EXPORTED TO OTHER COUNTRIES

30% ETHANOL FUEL

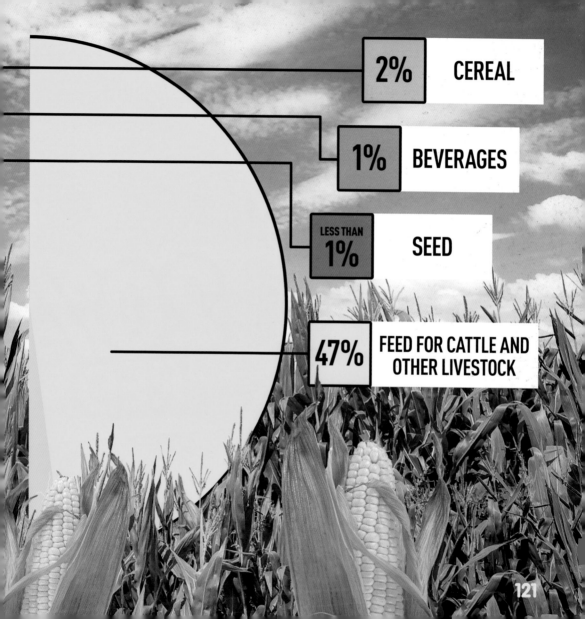

2% CEREAL

1% BEVERAGES

LESS THAN 1% SEED

47% FEED FOR CATTLE AND OTHER LIVESTOCK

121

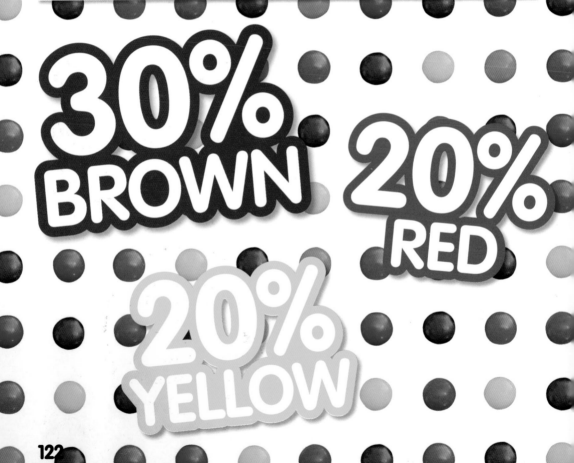

CANDY COLORS

Since 1941, people around the world have enjoyed M&M's candies. These candy-coated chocolates have been made in a variety of colors. Here's the percentage of each candy color you can expect to find in a bag of plain M&M's.

30% BROWN

20% RED

20% YELLOW

10% GREEN

10% ORANGE

10% BLUE

M&M's can be special-ordered in more than **20 DIFFERENT COLORS,** INCLUDING PINK, TEAL, SILVER, AND WHITE.

AMERICA'S **FAVORITE FELINES**

Every year, the Cat Fanciers' Association ranks the world's most popular purebreds. Curious to see which cute cats made the list? Enjoy these purr-fect feline stats!

#8 Abyssinian

#4 Ragdoll

#9 Sphynx

#5 British Shorthair

#10 Oriental

#6 American Shorthair

#7 Scottish Fold

#2

Persian

Cats spend **30–50%** of their day grooming themselves.

Exotic

#3

Maine Coon

#1

AFRICAN LANGUAGE LEADERS

How do you say hello? Around the continent of Africa, people speak over 2,000 different languages. Here's a breakdown of how many people use the top 10 African dialects and how to say "hello" in each!

ARABIC
150,000,000
NATIVE SPEAKERS
"MARHABAN"

HAUSA
34,000,000
NATIVE SPEAKERS
"SANNU"

People in Nigeria speak **OVER 500** different languages!

YORUBA
28,000,000
NATIVE SPEAKERS
"E N LE"

OROMO
26,000,000
NATIVE SPEAKERS
"ASHAM"

FULANI
25,000,000
NATIVE SPEAKERS
"SANNU"

AMHARIC
22,000,000
NATIVE SPEAKERS
"SALAAM"

IGBO
18,000,000
NATIVE SPEAKERS
"KEDU"

MALAGASY
18,000,000
NATIVE SPEAKERS
"MANAO AHOANA"

SOMALI
16,600,000
NATIVE SPEAKERS
"IS KA WARRAN"

SWAHILI
15,000,000
NATIVE SPEAKERS
"HABARI"

THE VERY HUNGRY **PANDA**

In the mountainous forests of China, black-and-white giant pandas roam the treetops. Their favorite thing to do? Eat! These bears have quite the appetite, spending half of every day eating. Chew on these giant panda facts.

PERCENT OF A PANDA'S DIET THAT IS BAMBOO:
99%

NUMBER OF DIFFERENT KINDS OF BAMBOO A PANDA WILL EAT:
MORE THAN
40

AMOUNT OF BAMBOO EATEN DAILY BY A PANDA:
28 POUNDS
(12.7 KG)

**AMOUNT OF TIME
A PANDA EATS:**

12
HOURS A DAY

**NUMBER
OF TEETH:**

42

WEIGHT AT BIRTH:

5 OUNCES
(142 G)

WEIGHT AS AN ADULT:

300 POUNDS
(136 KG)

COUNTING CARDS

From magic tricks to challenging games, there's no limit to the fun you can have with a deck of cards. People have been playing different kinds of card games since the 9th century. How many different ways can you shuffle a 52-card deck? More than you could mix up in a lifetime!

YOU CAN SHUFFLE A 52-CARD DECK

80,658,175,170,943,878,571,660, 636,856,403,766,975,289,505, 440,883,277,824,000,000,000,000

DIFFERENT WAYS!

80
UNVIGINTILLION
is how you say that
huge number!

That number is
so huge, it's statistically
unlikely that
ANY 2 DECKS
have **ever** been shuffled
the same way!

When you start reading a great book, it's hard to stop turning the pages! Here's how many words you'll read in the spellbinding Harry Potter series.

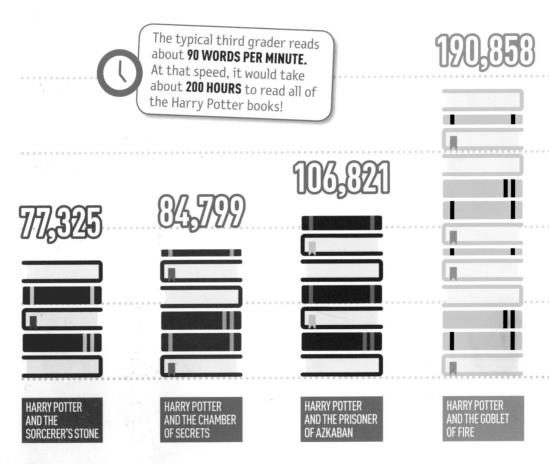

The typical third grader reads about **90 WORDS PER MINUTE.** At that speed, it would take about **200 HOURS** to read all of the Harry Potter books!

190,858

106,821

77,325

84,799

HARRY POTTER AND THE SORCERER'S STONE

HARRY POTTER AND THE CHAMBER OF SECRETS

HARRY POTTER AND THE PRISONER OF AZKABAN

HARRY POTTER AND THE GOBLET OF FIRE

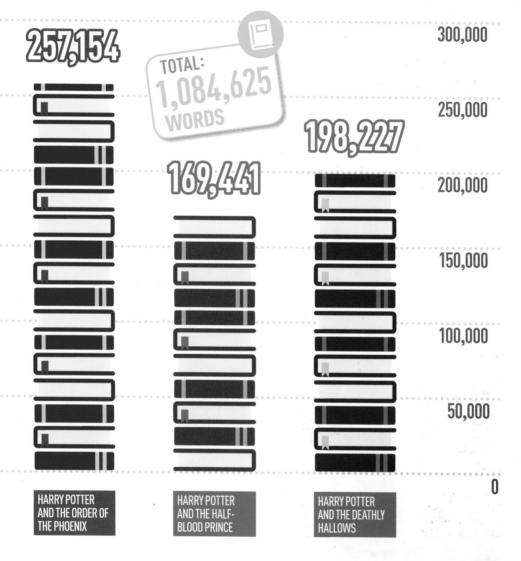

257,154

TOTAL: 1,084,625 WORDS

198,227

169,441

300,000

250,000

200,000

150,000

100,000

50,000

0

HARRY POTTER AND THE ORDER OF THE PHOENIX

HARRY POTTER AND THE HALF-BLOOD PRINCE

HARRY POTTER AND THE DEATHLY HALLOWS

TUNDRA TREK

Located just below the frozen Arctic and extending across the northern parts of North America, Europe, and Asia, the tundra is like a cold, dry desert. Welcome to the world's coldest biome!

TEMPERATURE:

-40°F to 64°F

(-40°C TO 18°C)

SUMMER LASTS FOR ONLY

2 MONTHS

IN THE TUNDRA.

THE ARCTIC FOX CAN SURVIVE IN TEMPERATURES AS LOW AS

-58°F. (-50°C)

CARIBOU (ALSO KNOWN AS REINDEER) CAN TRAVEL MORE THAN

800 MILES

(1,290 KM) ROUND-TRIP DURING THEIR YEARLY MIGRATION.

PRECIPITATION:

6–10 INCHES 💧

(150–250 MM) PER YEAR.
THAT'S LESS RAIN THAN IN MOST OF THE WORLD'S DESERTS!

MOST OF ALASKA AND

1/2

OF CANADA IS IN THE TUNDRA BIOME.

TEMPERATURES ARE BELOW 32°F (0°C) FOR

6–10 MONTHS

OF THE YEAR.

HOW DO YOU TELL STORIES AND CHANGE LIVES WITH DATA AND DESIGN?

MEET >>>

AMY BALLIETT CAN SHOW YOU HOW!

Q: WHAT DO YOU DO?

A: I started a company that creates infographics! We take data and illustrate the information using accurate visuals to tell a story without relying on text.

Q: HOW DOES YOUR WORK CHANGE THE WORLD?

A: I believe that proper visual communication can create extremely positive change. Visual content can inspire action globally because visual languages are universal. By sharing accurate data and showing how someone can impact that data through action, great things can happen.

›› AMY BALLIETT, INFOGRAPHICS ENTREPRENEUR

Q: WHAT'S THE COOLEST DISCOVERY YOU'VE MADE?

A: Everyone has extremely busy lives and picks and chooses the information they take in every day. That's why I help organizations speak visually to speed up their message of change. For example, we once worked with a charity that was struggling to explain their mission. We designed a poster that visually showed who they were and why they mattered. It helped them reach new people and change a lot of lives for the better. Watching how visualizing information can quickly grab attention and change minds has been amazing.

Q: HOW CAN I THINK LIKE A DATA DESIGNER?

A: Think visually! Immerse yourself in numbers and identify the best ways to display your findings. Then, share your ideas with the people around you!

9%
AGRICULTURE AND LIVESTOCK

12%
COMMERCIAL AND RESIDENTIAL

Help the planet and get some exercise at the same time! Walk or bike instead of riding in a car. Even a **1-MILE** (1.6-KM) car trip can put **1 POUND** (.45 KG) of CO_2 into the atmosphere.

21%
MANUFACTURING

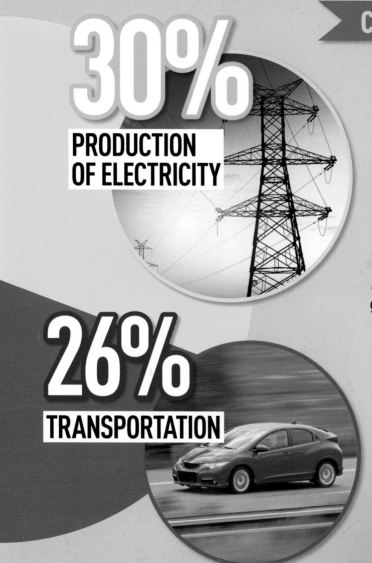

30%

PRODUCTION OF ELECTRICITY

26%

TRANSPORTATION

Climate change is a hot problem. The 10 hottest years on record have all happened since 1998. Why is the temperature rising? Greenhouse gases like carbon dioxide, methane, and nitrous oxide are being released into our atmosphere. Emissions grew faster from 2000 to 2010 than they did in the previous 30 years. Find out where these greenhouse gases are coming from on this chart.

FAMOUS FAILURES

Think a big flub is the end of the road? Think again! Read on to find out how these accomplished scientists, authors, and entertainers bounced back from blunders and went on to become super successful.

12

Number of times J. K. ROWLING'S books were rejected before *HARRY POTTER AND THE SORCERER'S STONE* was published. The entire Harry Potter series has now sold more than 450 MILLION COPIES WORLDWIDE—making J. K. Rowling the first author to earn over a billion dollars from books and films.

LESS THAN 10%

Percentage of his paintings VINCENT VAN GOGH sold during his lifetime. He painted over 900 PAINTINGS, including famous pieces like "CAFÉ TERRACE AT NIGHT."

27

Number of times DR. SEUSS'S first book was turned down by book publishers. He went on to write and illustrate 44 FAMOUS CHILDREN'S BOOKS.

30

Age at which STEVE JOBS left Apple, his own company. He later worked his way back to Apple and made history by leading the teams that invented the iPOD, iPHONE, AND iPAD.

5

Number of elections that ABRAHAM LINCOLN lost before becoming PRESIDENT OF THE UNITED STATES.

$2.9 BILLION

OPRAH WINFREY'S net worth. She was once fired from her job as a reporter and told that she wasn't fit for TV.

AND THE AWARD GOES TO ...

If you're a movie buff, you've probably seen the Academy Awards! Organized by the Academy of Motion Picture Arts and Sciences, Oscars are awarded to the best movies, actors, and directors each year. Here are the numbers behind the golden statues.

FIRST AWARD CEREMONY:
5/6/1929

AGE OF YOUNGEST OSCAR WINNER:
10 YEARS OLD

Tatum O'Neal won Best Supporting Actress in 1974.

NUMBER OF PEOPLE IN THE U.S. WHO WATCHED THE 2017 CEREMONY ON TV:
32.9 MILLION

2

WEIGHT OF OSCAR STATUETTE:

8.5 POUNDS
(3.9 KG)

That's as heavy as a bowling ball!

AVERAGE LENGTH OF ACCEPTANCE SPEECH:

45 SECONDS

In 1943, Best Actress winner Greer Garson gave the longest Oscars acceptance speech ever: **5 MINUTES AND 30 SECONDS!**

What about the shortest speech? In 1991, Best Supporting Actor winner Joe Pesci said just **6 WORDS:** "It was my privilege. Thank you!"

NUMBER OF OSCARS AWARDED FROM 1929 TO 2017:

3,048

Garrett McNamara made surfing history when he tackled a giant wave off the coast of Portugal. Just how big was this monster wave? Read on to find out!

WAVE HEIGHT:

100 FEET
(30 M)

THAT'S AS TALL AS A STACK OF
5 GIRAFFES!

Garrett has been surfing since he was 11 YEARS OLD.

CLIMBING **KILIMANJARO**

Standing tall above the plains of Tanzania, Mount Kilimanjaro is the highest mountain in Africa. Ready to make the climb? Here's everything you need to know!

NUMBER OF PEOPLE WHO TRY TO CLIMB EACH YEAR:

25,000

HEIGHT:

19,340 FEET

(5,895 M)

AGE OF OLDEST PERSON TO EVER SUMMIT:

87

FASTEST ASCENT:

6 HOURS 42 MINUTES 24 SECONDS

ANIMALS YOU MIGHT SEE ALONG THE WAY:

ELEPHANTS, LEOPARDS, BLUE MONKEYS

YEAR OF FIRST RECORDED SUMMIT:

1889

FASTEST ROUND-TRIP:

8 HOURS 27 MINUTES

LAST MAJOR ERUPTION:

360,000 YEARS AGO

NUMBER OF VOLCANIC CONES:

3

(2 ARE EXTINCT)

ALMOST EVERY KIND OF ECOSYSTEM IS FOUND ON MOUNT KILIMANJARO:

CULTIVATED LAND, RAIN FOREST, SHRUBLAND, MOORLAND, ALPINE DESERT, AND AN ARCTIC SUMMIT.

PASTA POWER

Spaghetti, rigatoni, macaroni! Pasta is an Italian specialty, but Americans love to eat it, too. Which country chows down on more pasta? Hope you're hungry—it's a saucy smackdown!

ITALY

YEAR FIRST ITALIAN PASTA FACTORY OPENED:

1740 IN VENICE, ITALY

AMOUNT OF PASTA MADE IN ITALY EACH YEAR:

2.75 MILLION TONS (2.5 million t)

AMOUNT OF PASTA EATEN BY THE AVERAGE ITALIAN EACH YEAR:

51 POUNDS (23.1 kg)

WINNER!

USA

THERE ARE MORE THAN 600 DIFFERENT PASTA SHAPES MADE WORLDWIDE!

YEAR FIRST AMERICAN PASTA FACTORY OPENED:

1848 IN BROOKLYN, NEW YORK

AMOUNT OF PASTA MADE IN AMERICA EACH YEAR:

1.9 MILLION TONS (1.7 million t)

AMOUNT OF PASTA EATEN BY
THE AVERAGE AMERICAN EACH YEAR:

15.5 POUNDS (7 kg)

SAVE THE BEES, PLEASE!

Next time you sit down to a delicious meal, thank the bees! Honeybees are responsible for pollinating 80 percent of the world's plants, including the foods we eat every day. Unfortunately, pesticides, habitat loss, and climate change are challenging bees in a big way. Buzz through these fast facts and find out how you can help.

70%

Percent of top human food crops pollinated by bees, including fruits, vegetables, and nuts

6 MILLION

Number of U.S. hives in 1947

2.4 MILLION

Number of U.S. hives in 2008

That's **60%** fewer bees!

YOU CAN HELP!
Plant bee-friendly flowers in your garden and stop using chemicals and pesticides in your yard.

7

Number of bee species placed on the endangered species list in 2016

300 MILLION

Number of flowers 1 bee colony can pollinate each day

151

THE HEIGHT OF **FLIGHT**

Thanks to advances in aviation technology, humans can fly higher than ever! Here's the altitude of different aircraft and spacecraft.

250 MILES (402.3 KM)

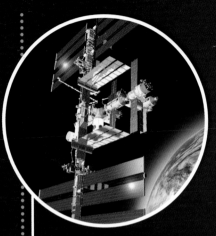

INTERNATIONAL SPACE STATION
248 MILES (399.1 KM)

200 MILES (321.8 KM)

YURI GAGARIN,
THE FIRST HUMAN IN OUTER SPACE
187 MILES (300.9 KM)

150 MILES (241.4 KM)

SPACESHIPTWO
EXPERIMENTAL ROCKET-POWERED AIRCRAFT
69 MILES (111 KM)

HIGH-ALTITUDE
WEATHER BALLOONS
32 MILES (51.5 KM)

HIGHEST MANNED
HOT AIR BALLOON
13 MILES (20.9 KM)

PASSENGER AIRPLANE
8 MILES (12.9 KM)

100 MILES (160.9 KM)

50 MILES (80.4 KM)

0 MILES

LIFE ON THE ICE

Emperor penguins live in Antarctica, one of the coldest places on the planet. Spending their entire lives on the ice and in the frigid water, these flightless birds have learned how to survive. Take a peek inside the chilly life of an emperor penguin.

TEMPERATURE ON ANTARCTIC ICE WITH WIND CHILL:

-76°F

(-60°C)

TIME EMPEROR PENGUINS CAN STAY UNDERWATER:

20 MINUTES

SWIMMING SPEED:

4.6 MILES AN HOUR
(7.4 KM/H)

DIVE DEPTH:

1,850 FEET (564 M)

THAT'S DEEPER THAN THE WILLIS TOWER IN CHICAGO IS TALL!

WEIGHT:

UP TO 88 POUNDS
(40 KG)

DISTANCE A FEMALE WILL TRAVEL TO FIND FOOD:

SOME 50 MILES
(80 KM)

TOURIST TO-DO LIST

The world is full of incredible, unforgettable sights! But which ones are the most popular? Tour the globe and see some of the world's top tourist destinations.

NIAGARA FALLS
NEW YORK, UNITED STATES AND ONTARIO, CANADA
VISITORS PER YEAR:
22,000,000

You'll need your raincoat for this trip! About six million cubic feet (169,900 m^3) of water pour over the falls every minute, creating clouds of mist that can soak visitors.

THE ZÓCALO
MEXICO CITY, MEXICO
VISITORS PER YEAR:
85,000,000

You can see parades, concerts, fairs, and art at this historic public square.

TIMES SQUARE
NEW YORK CITY, UNITED STATES
VISITORS PER YEAR: 50,000,000

Happy New Year! Over a million people gather at Times Square to watch the ball drop on New Year's Eve.

MEIJI JINGU SHRINE
TOKYO, JAPAN
VISITORS PER YEAR:
30,000,000
More than 100,000 trees surround this peaceful Shinto shrine in the middle of busy Tokyo.

GRAND BAZAAR
ISTANBUL, TURKEY
VISITORS PER YEAR: 91,250,000
This majestic marketplace was built in the 15th century!

GREAT WALL OF CHINA
CHINA
VISITORS PER YEAR:
10,720,000
(Badaling and Mutianyu areas)
China's first emperor started building this famous wall in the 3rd century B.C. Today, the wall's many sections span over 5,000 miles (8,046 km) total.

157

TORTOISE VS. HARE

Have you heard the story of the tortoise and the hare?
This favorite folktale pits the lumbering tortoise against the speedy hare. Which one would win in real life? Read on to find out!

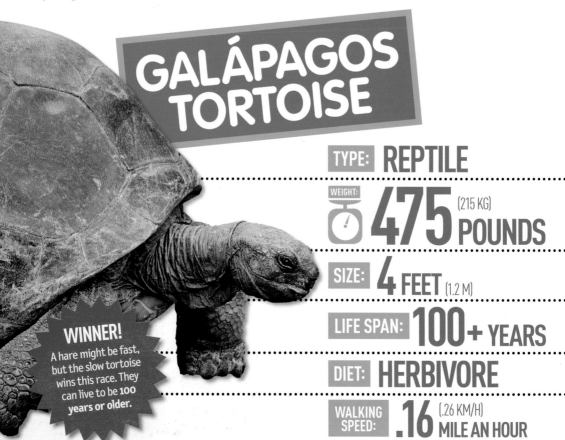

GALÁPAGOS TORTOISE

TYPE: REPTILE

WEIGHT: 475 POUNDS (215 KG)

SIZE: 4 FEET (1.2 M)

LIFE SPAN: 100+ YEARS

DIET: HERBIVORE

WALKING SPEED: .16 MILE AN HOUR (.26 KM/H)

WINNER!
A hare might be fast, but the slow tortoise wins this race. They can live to be 100 years or older.

SNOWSHOE HARE

An adult hare can travel up to **10 FEET** (3 m) in a single leap!

TYPE: MAMMAL

WEIGHT: 2-4 POUNDS (0.9–1.8 KG)

SIZE: 16-20 INCHES (41.3–51.8 CM)

LIFE SPAN: 1 YEAR OR LESS

DIET: HERBIVORE

SPRINT SPEED: UP TO 27 MILES AN HOUR (43.5 KM/H)

GIANT GENERAL SHERMAN

If you visit Sequoia and Kings Canyon National Parks in California, you could meet General Sherman! Yes, it's a tree, and it happens to be one of the oldest, widest, and tallest trees on Earth. How does this giant sequoia measure up? Let's find out!

ESTIMATED AGE

2,300–2,700 YEARS

DIAMETER 60 FEET
(18 M) ABOVE BASE

17.5 FEET
[5.3 M]

HEIGHT OF FIRST LARGE BRANCH ABOVE BASE

130 FEET
[39.6 M]

DIAMETER OF LARGEST BRANCH

6.8 FEET
[2.1 M]

TRUNK MASS

2,472,000 POUNDS

(1,124,280 KG)

General Sherman is about as tall as the **STATUE OF LIBERTY!**

HEIGHT

275 FEET

(83.8 M)

DIAMETER AT BASE

36.5 FEET

(11.1 M)

CIRCUMFERENCE AT GROUND

102.6 FEET

(31.3 M)

GENERAL SHERMAN

THIRST QUENCHERS

What's in your cup? Researchers asked more than 11,000 high school kids to report the drinks they had enjoyed in the past week. Here's a look at what they're drinking!

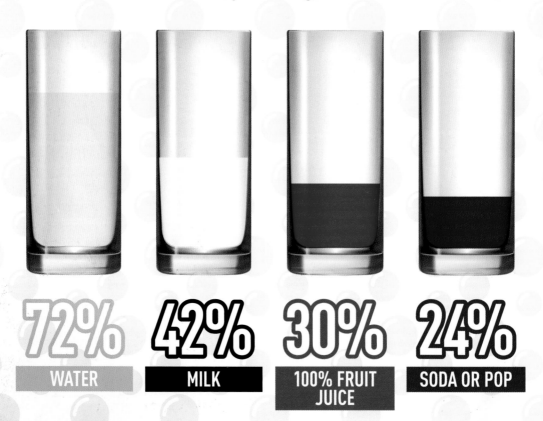

72% WATER

42% MILK

30% 100% FRUIT JUICE

24% SODA OR POP

Craving a juice or soda? Don't go overboard! The average American kid gets about **270** calories from sugary soda and juice each day. That adds up to a total of about **7 TRILLION** calories each year.

17%
LEMONADE, SWEET TEA,
OR OTHER SUGARY NON-CARBONATED DRINKS

16%
SPORTS DRINK

7%
DIET SODA OR POP

5%
ENERGY DRINK

4 states in America have more cows than people living there. Is yours one of them?

IN SOUTH DAKOTA, THERE ARE

2 COWS...

... FOR EVERY

1 PERSON

MONTANA,
NORTH DAKOTA,
and WYOMING also
have more bovine
residents than
human. Moo!

DWARF PLANET **PLUTO**

Since its discovery in 1930, Pluto was known as the smallest planet in our solar system. As astronomers discovered more Pluto-size objects, they decided to create a new category just for these smaller planets: dwarf planets! Here are the big numbers behind this pint-size planet.

TEMPERATURE:

-375°F to -400°F

(-226°C to -240°C)

SIZE:

1,400

(2,300 KM)

MILES WIDE

THAT'S ABOUT HALF THE WIDTH OF THE UNITED STATES!

TIME TO ORBIT AROUND THE SUN:

248

YEARS

1 DAY on Pluto is about **6½ DAYS** on Earth.

NUMBER OF MOONS:

5

A person who weighs **100 POUNDS** (45 kg) would weigh **7 POUNDS** (3.2 kg) on Pluto.

MOST RECENT MOON DISCOVERY:

2012

DISTANCE FROM THE SUN:

3.6 (5.8 BILLION KM) **BILLION MILES**

THAT'S 40 TIMES AS FAR FROM THE SUN AS EARTH IS.

GO ASK GOOGLE

When you have a question, where do you go to find the answer?
Google it! Serving up answers to trillions of queries every year, Google's
search engine is a go-to place to find all kinds of information on the
Internet. Here are the top Google search topics in the U.S. for 2015 and 2016.

#1 SEARCHED DRINK:

Water

#1 SEARCHED SONG:

"Happy Birthday"

#1 SEARCHED DOG:

Husky

#1 SEARCHED RECIPE:

Green Bean Casserole 🔍

#1 SEARCHED FOOD:

Pizza 🔍

Got more questions?
Ask away: Google answers
40,000 SEARCH QUERIES
every second!

#1 SEARCHED VIDEO GAME:

Pokémon Go 🔍

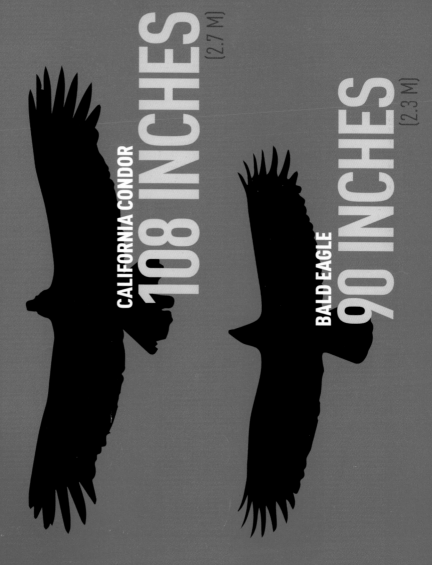

WIDE WINGSPANS

These birds have incredible wingspans! Compare the wing measurements of these North American birds.

CALIFORNIA CONDOR
108 INCHES (2.7 M)

BALD EAGLE
90 INCHES (2.3 M)

BROWN PELICAN

84 INCHES [2.1 M]

GREATER FLAMINGO

60 INCHES [1.5 M]

RED-TAILED HAWK

50 INCHES [1.3 M]

PEREGRINE FALCON

44 INCHES [1.1 M]

The **CALIFORNIA CONDOR** is the largest flying bird in North America. As of 2015, there were only **268** living in the wild.

AWESOME AURORA ALTITUDES

The aurora borealis is a magical sight. As the temperature on the sun's surface rises and falls, particles of plasma escape from sunspots and are thrown into space. When these solar winds reach Earth, they can cause a rainbow of light to dance through the night sky at higher elevations. How high are these colors? Read on to find out!

BLUE LIGHTS
UP TO
60 MILES
(97 KM)

Cave paintings may show aurora sightings up to **30,000** years ago!

GREEN LIGHTS
UP TO
150 MILES
(241 KM)

PURPLE AND VIOLET LIGHTS
ABOVE
60 MILES
(97 KM)

RED LIGHTS
ABOVE
150 MILES
(241 KM)

The best place to view the lights? Go north! **Alaska, northern Canada, Norway, Sweden,** and **Finland** are aurora hot spots.

You can also see auroras in southern areas like **Antarctica, Chile, Argentina, New Zealand,** and **Australia!**

HOT AND COLD

Pack your swimsuit and your parka, too!
If you travel the world, you'll find all different kinds of weather. Explore the hottest and coldest temperatures on Earth, from the blazing hot deserts of Africa to the subzero ice of Antarctica!

EUROPE

118.4°F	-72.6°F
(48°C)	(-58.1°C)
ATHENS	UST-SHCHUGER
GREECE	KOMI REPUBLIC, RUSSIA
JULY 10, 1977	DECEMBER 31, 1978

WINNER!
Hottest air temperature ever recorded on Earth!

NORTH AMERICA

134°F	-81.4°F
(56.7°C)	(-63°C)
FURNACE CREEK RANCH	SNAG
CALIFORNIA, U.S.A.	YUKON TERRITORY, CANADA
JULY 10, 1913	FEBRUARY 3, 1947

SOUTH AMERICA

120°F	-27°F
(48.9°C)	(-32.8°C)
RIVADAVIA	SARMIENTO
SALTA PROVINCE, ARGENTINA	CHUBUT PROVINCE, ARGENTINA
DECEMBER 11, 1905	JUNE 1, 1907

ASIA

129°F	-90°F	-90°F
(54°C)	(-67.8°C)	(-67.8°C)
TIRAT ZVI	VERKHOYANSK	OYMYAKON
ISRAEL	SAKHA REPUBLIC, RUSSIA	SAKHA REPUBLIC, RUSSIA
JUNE 21, 1942	FEBRUARY 5, 1892	FEBRUARY 5, 1892
	AND JULY 5, 1892	

OCEANIA

123°F	-14°F
(50.7°C)	(-25.6°C)
OODNADATTA	RANFURLY
SOUTH AUSTRALIA, AUSTRALIA	OTAGO, NEW ZEALAND
JANUARY 2, 1960	JULY 17, 1903

AFRICA

131°F	-11°F
(55°C)	(-23.9°C)
KEBILI	IFRANE
TUNISIA	MOROCCO
JULY 7, 1931	FEBRUARY 11, 1935

ANTARCTICA

59°F	-135.8°F
(15°C)	(-93.2°C)
VANDA STATION	EAST ANTARCTICA
MAY 1, 1974	AUGUST 10, 2010

WINNER!
Coldest air temperature ever recorded on Earth!

Every time you catch a whiff of your favorite food, your nose is keeping you in the know. Using your sense of smell, your nose and brain can tell the differences between the scent molecules that make up the world around you. But can you smell better than your pup? It's a sniffer smackdown!

A HUMAN HAS

5-6 MILLION

SCENT CELLS IN THEIR NOSE.

Your nose can smell at least
1 TRILLION
different scents!

A DOG HAS

220 MILLION

SCENT CELLS IN ITS NOSE.

WHAT'S YOUR **TYPE?**

Everyone's blood is made of the same basic elements, but not all blood is alike. There are 4 main common blood types. If a person needs to use donated blood, the donated blood can react with their body's immune system if it's not the right type. This diagram shows which types of blood are compatible with each other.

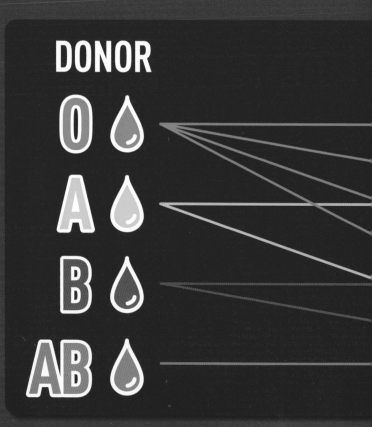

DONOR

GROUP O can donate red blood cells to anybody. It's the universal donor.

GROUP A can donate red blood cells to A's and AB's.

GROUP B can donate red blood cells to B's and AB's.

GROUP AB can donate to other AB's, but can receive from all others.

RECIPIENT

O

A

B

AB

GLOBAL ROAD TRIP

Hop in the car! It's time for a road trip. But this isn't your ordinary drive to the beach. We're going all the way around the world! Here's how long it would take to drive around the Earth at its widest point, the Equator.

EARTH'S CIRCUMFERENCE AT EQUATOR:

24,874 MILES

(40,030 KM)

TIME IT WOULD TAKE YOU TO DRIVE ALL THE WAY AROUND THE WORLD GOING 65 MILES AN HOUR: (104.6 KM/H)

383 HOURS

THAT'S LIKE DRIVING ACROSS THE UNITED STATES
8 TIMES!

You'd need an epic playlist for this road trip:
7,640
3-MINUTE SONGS
to be exact!

BOARD GAME BASICS

It's time for game night! And, speaking of time, some of the most popular board games ever invented have been around for a long time. Centuries, in fact! Let's move our pawns through board game history—and discover some fun facts to share during your next game session.

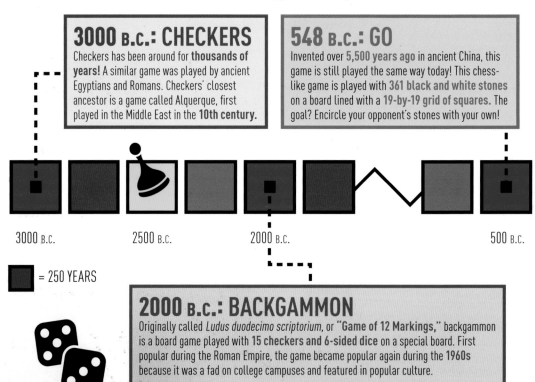

3000 B.C.: CHECKERS
Checkers has been around for **thousands of years!** A similar game was played by ancient Egyptians and Romans. Checkers' closest ancestor is a game called Alquerque, first played in the Middle East in the **10th century.**

548 B.C.: GO
Invented over **5,500 years ago** in ancient China, this game is still played the same way today! This chess-like game is played with **361 black and white stones** on a board lined with a **19-by-19 grid of squares.** The goal? Encircle your opponent's stones with your own!

3000 B.C.   2500 B.C.   2000 B.C.   500 B.C.

■ = 250 YEARS

2000 B.C.: BACKGAMMON
Originally called *Ludus duodecimo scriptorium*, or "**Game of 12 Markings,**" backgammon is a board game played with **15 checkers and 6-sided dice** on a special board. First popular during the Roman Empire, the game became popular again during the **1960s** because it was a fad on college campuses and featured in popular culture.

1904: THE LANDLORD'S GAME

(Or, Monopoly!) Have you heard of the Landlord's Game? Over **1 billion people** around the world have played it! Lizzie Magie, one of the first American board game designers, sold her game idea to Parker Brothers in 1935. The company rereleased it as—you guessed it—Monopoly! The game is currently made in **47 languages** and sold in **114 countries**.

700: MANCALA

Originally played with seeds in Africa, mancala isn't just one game. There are over **800 different versions of this game** played around the world!

1995: SETTLERS OF CATAN

One of the first modern European board games to become popular in the United States, Settlers of Catan was created by a dental technician in Germany who invented the game in his basement! Over **24 million copies** of Catan have been sold.

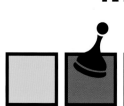

0   500   1000   1500   2000

1475: CHESS

While earlier versions were played in India as far back as A.D. **280**, the game we know and love today was developed around **1475** in Italy and Spain. The game spread around Europe, and the first modern chess tournament was held in London in **1851**.

1948: SCRABBLE

Originally called Lexiko and Criss Cross Words, Scrabble was invented by Alfred Mosher Butts, an architect who lost his job. The first Scrabble games were handmade, with each letter tile stamped by hand. The game didn't catch on until Macy's department store started selling it. Scrabble became an instant hit! Today, Scrabble is found in **3 out of 5 American homes**.

ANIMATED A-LISTERS

Animated movies are anything but *Frozen*—in fact, they're taking over the box office charts! From '90s' classics to new favorites, here are the top 10 animated movies of all time, based on global box office revenue.

*Box office figures have been adjusted for inflation.
*This data is current as of May 2016.

#1 THE LION KING 1994
$775.5 MILLION

#2 SHREK 2 2004
$618.1 MILLION

#3 FINDING NEMO 2003
$536 MILLION

#4 ALADDIN 1992
$456.2 MILLION

#5 TOY STORY 3 2010

$454.1 MILLION

#6 MONSTERS, INC. 2001

$429.3 MILLION

#7 FROZEN 2013

$427 MILLION

#8 TOY STORY 2 1999

$416.1 MILLION

#9 SHREK 2001

$411.4 MILLION

#10 SHREK THE THIRD 2007

$408 MILLION

A GIANT SQUID'S EYE
MEASURES ABOUT

10 INCHES

(25 CM)

IN DIAMETER.

186

THAT'S AS BIG AS A
BEACH BALL!

They have the **BIGGEST EYES** in the animal kingdom!

VEGGIE VALUES

Have you eaten your vegetables today?
If you're like 9 out of 10 American kids, you don't eat the daily recommended amount of veggies. Researchers surveyed 500 kids to find out which ones they like and eat the most often. We're serving up the statistics below!

23%
OF KIDS LIKE CARROTS

70%
of vegetables eaten in America are served during dinner.

29%
OF KIDS LIKE BROCCOLI

Girls' favorite vegetable!

12%
OF KIDS LIKE
POTATOES

32%
OF KIDS LIKE
CORN

→ Boys' favorite vegetable!

17%
OF KIDS LIKE
GREEN BEANS

11%
OF KIDS LIKE
TOMATOES

What time is it? The answer depends on where you are! Across the Earth, there are 38 different time zones in use. Each time zone is offset from Coordinated Universal Time, the world's time standard that is synchronized with solar time. Take a trip through the world's time zones.

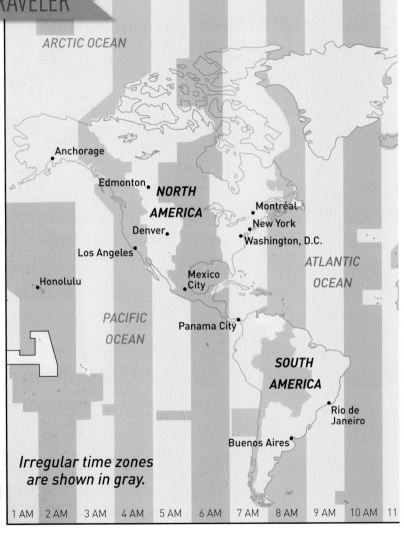

Number of main time zones spaced 1 hour apart:

24

Number of additional time zones:

18

Irregular time zones are shown in gray.

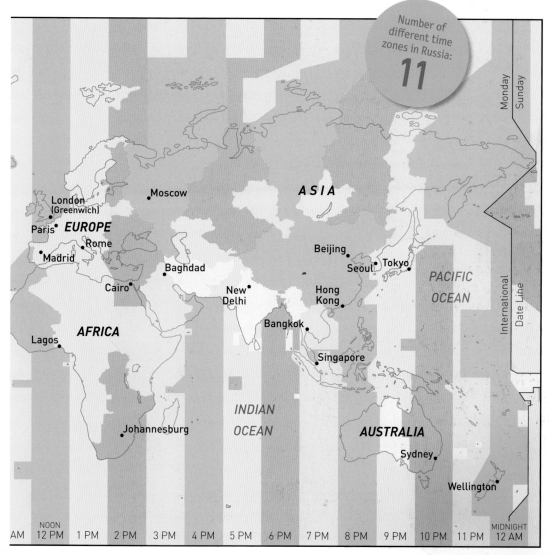

Number of different time zones in Russia: **11**

Monday | Sunday

ASIA

Moscow

London (Greenwich)
Paris • *EUROPE*
Rome
Madrid

Beijing
Seoul • Tokyo

Baghdad

Cairo

New Delhi

Hong Kong

PACIFIC OCEAN

International Date Line

Bangkok

AFRICA

Lagos

Singapore

INDIAN OCEAN

AUSTRALIA

Johannesburg

Sydney

Wellington

AM | 12 PM NOON | 1 PM | 2 PM | 3 PM | 4 PM | 5 PM | 6 PM | 7 PM | 8 PM | 9 PM | 10 PM | 11 PM | 12 AM MIDNIGHT

What's in your skin? About 1.6 trillion skin cells! Your skin is made of several layers, and they're constantly shedding to make room for new cells. Just how many skin cells are you losing every year? You might be grossed out by the number!

EVERY YEAR, YOU SHED

500 MILLION

SKIN CELLS. TOGETHER, THOSE CELLS WEIGH MORE THAN

8 POUNDS.

(3.6 KG)

THAT'S ABOUT AS HEAVY AS

A GALLON (3.8 L)
OF MILK!

NUMBER OF STRIPES ON FLAG:

13

ONE FOR EACH OF THE ORIGINAL 13 COLONIES

NUMBER OF STARS ON CURRENT FLAG:

50

ONE FOR EACH OF THE 50 UNITED STATES

NUMBER OF STARS ON ORIGINAL FLAG:

13

DATE FIRST AMERICAN FLAG WAS ADOPTED:

JUNE 14, 1777

DATE CURRENT AMERICAN FLAG WAS ADOPTED:

JULY 4, 1960

Flying high above our schools and monuments, and even on the moon, the American flag tells the story of how our country came to be. Read on to learn more about the meaning behind the star-spangled banner.

DATE FIRST AMERICAN FLAG WAS PLACED ON THE MOON:

JULY 1969

Did you know a teen designed the American flag we fly today? **17-YEAR-OLD** Robert G. Heft designed the current **50-STAR** flag in 1958 as a high school project.

YEARS CURRENT FLAG DESIGN HAS BEEN IN USE:

57

THE LONGEST OF ANY VERSION

MEAT
Ounces

VEGETABLES

MEET **NATHAN YAU,** STATISTICIAN

Beef

1.14

Chicke

0.94

Seafoo

0.34

Turkey

0.18

Veal

0.07

Lamb

0.04

Legumes

0.15

Bananas

Corn Flour

4.13

0.30

Rice

0.18

elon

Hominy and G

0.12

Grapes

0.02

Corn Starch

0.11

Strawberries

0.01

Oats

0.11

Avocado

0.00

Rye Flour

0.05

0.03

EVERYONE CAN LEARN FROM DATA!

Statistician Nathan Yau thinks that everyone can learn a thing or two from data. That's why he made a website that helps people understand data and how it affects their everyday lives. "Data provides a different point of view that you can't quite get from just looking out your window," Nathan says. "It lets you learn about people, places, and things in great detail and at a large scale." By using colorful charts, graphs, and interactive graphics, Nathan helps people discover patterns in data that might have been invisible if you were just looking at the raw numbers. Want to know how to think like Nathan? Here are his top three tips!

196

HERE ARE NATHAN'S TIPS!

1 **BE CURIOUS.** DATA IS ALL AROUND US! LOOK AROUND AND SEE WHAT INFORMATION YOU CAN FIND IN YOUR EVERYDAY LIFE.

2 **MAKE IT INTERESTING.** DATA HAS A REP FOR BEING DRY, BUT WHEN YOU PRESENT IT IN THE RIGHT WAY, PEOPLE ARE WILLING TO SPEND A LOT MORE TIME WITH THE "BORING" NUMBERS!

3 **JUST DO IT!** AND START TO MAKE YOUR OWN CHARTS AND GRAPHS. IT MIGHT BE A CHALLENGE AT FIRST, BUT **HAVE FUN WITH IT!**

Whole
0.63

Ameri

0.19

2 pct

0.14

Ice (

0.07

Itali

0.06

1 pct

0.05

Skim

0.04

FUNNY FESTIVALS

Whether you want to get dirty, talk like a pirate, or nibble on some fine cheeses, there's a festival out there for everyone! Check out these unique celebrations from around the globe.

Boryeong Mud Festival in South Korea draws more than

3 MILLION PEOPLE

who gather to soak in mud-filled plastic pools, run a mud race, and get their faces painted with colored mud.

Set sail for the Pirates Week Festival in the Cayman Islands, where

3 SHIPS

filled with people in pirate costumes sail into the town harbor to get the party started.

In Spain, **20,000 PEOPLE** gather for La Tomatina, where the main attraction is a huge food fight with over **100 TONS** (90.7 t) of tomatoes.

At the Wisconsin Cheese Festival, visitors can watch artists carve sculptures out of **40-POUND** (18.1-kg) blocks of cheddar.

In the Netherlands, over **5,000 PEOPLE** get together once a year for Redhead Days. Non-redheads can come, too!

MUSEUM MASTERPIECES

Scattered throughout the world's museums, these amazing artworks are unforgettable. But do you know how long these works of art have been around? Feast your eyes on the world's most famous paintings and find out when these masterpieces were created.

"MONA LISA"

Leonardo da Vinci painted this portrait of a softly smiling woman. Since then, it has become the most well-known painting in the world. Currently on display at the Louvre Museum in Paris, this work is visited by over **8.8 MILLION** art lovers each year.

CIRCA 1503

"THE CREATION OF ADAM"

Michelangelo's masterpiece is a part of the massive mural he painted on the ceiling of the Sistine Chapel, within the official home of the Pope in Vatican City. The entire mural measures **132 FEET** (40.2 M) long, **44 FEET** (13.4 M) wide, and **68 FEET** (20.7 M) tall.

1508–1512

1889

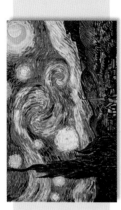

"THE STARRY NIGHT"
Painted by Vincent van Gogh in JUNE 1889, this spectacular summer night sky is now in the permanent collection at the Museum of Modern Art in New York City.

1893

"THE SCREAM"
This famous painting is actually many famous paintings! Edvard Munch created 4 DIFFERENT VERSIONS of "The Scream." In 2012, one version sold for $119.9 MILLION. Two other versions of "The Scream" have been targeted by thieves, being stolen from museums in 1994 and 2004. Both paintings were eventually found and returned.

1930

"AMERICAN GOTHIC"
Inspired by a farmhouse in Iowa, Grant Wood painted this portrait of rural Americans in 1930. It's now one of the most recognizable artworks of the 20TH CENTURY. Wood entered "American Gothic" in an art competition and won the bronze medal—and $300. That would be over $4,300 today!

1931

"THE PERSISTENCE OF MEMORY"
Who could forget these twisted timepieces? Salvador Dali's surreal world comes to life in this famous painting of melting clocks. First shown in 1932 and again in 1934, the painting has been at the Museum of Modern Art in New York City ever since.

PIE CHARTS

From pumpkin pie at Thanksgiving to apple pies on the Fourth of July, pies are a dessert that can be enjoyed year-round! Here's a, well, *pie chart* showing the percentage of people who ranked each flavor in their top 3 favorite pies!

47%
APPLE

37%
PUMPKIN

32%
CHOCOLATE CREAM

27%
CHERRY

24% PECAN

24% LEMON MERINGUE

21% BLUEBERRY

27% of people surveyed think their mom makes the best pies.

18% KEY LIME

16% PEACH

SEEING **STARS**

On a clear night, your eyes can see about 3,000 stars in Earth's sky. That may sound like a lot, but it's only a fraction of how many stars are really out there. How many stars, exactly? Read on to find out!

OUR UNIVERSE CONTAINS MORE THAN

100 BILLION GALAXIES.

EACH OF THOSE GALAXIES MAY HAVE MORE THAN

100 BILLION STARS!

BEST FRIENDS FOREVER!
ABOUT
75% OF STARS
ARE PART OF A PAIR OF 2 STARS
THAT ORBIT EACH OTHER.

BUSY BURROWERS

Can you dig it? These crafty animals build their homes underground, digging vast networks of tunnels, holes, and shelters deep below the soil. You won't believe what's going on beneath your feet!

BEAVERS BUILD BURROWS THAT HAVE

2 ROOMS:

1 FOR DRYING OFF AFTER SWIMMING IN THE WATER, AND 1 WHERE THE BEAVERS LIVE.

GROUNDHOGS' BURROWS CAN BE UP TO

46 FEET

(14 M) LONG AND
5 FEET (1.5 M) UNDERGROUND.

BLACK-TAILED PRAIRIE DOGS DIG GIANT BURROWS THAT CAN HOUSE UP TO

400,000
ANIMALS.

A MEERKAT BURROW CAN HAVE UP TO

90 ENTRANCES

WITH TUNNELS THAT EXTEND
6.5 FEET (2 M) INTO THE SOIL.

THAT'S A
BURROW!

THE PERFECT PB&J

There's nothing like a classic peanut butter and jelly sandwich for lunch. But how do you craft the perfect PB&J? Researchers surveyed sandwich lovers to figure out their favorite ingredients. Here's a jam-packed pie chart with the results!

3%
ORANGE MARMALADE

4%
APRICOT

5%
BLUEBERRY

21%
RASPBERRY

* THIS CHART ADDS UP TO MORE THAN 100% DUE TO ROUNDING.

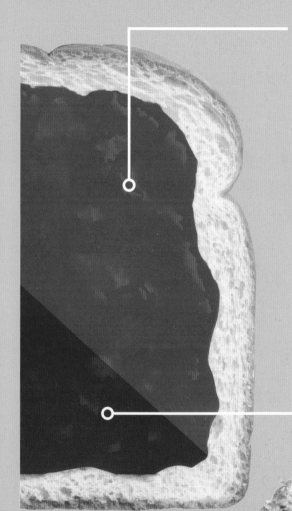

37%
STRAWBERRY

31%
GRAPE

When it comes to crust, there's no contest:
80%
of people prefer their PB&J with crust!

BIOME BASICS

What's the weather like where you live? Different parts of the world have different weather patterns and different animals and plants that live there. These communities of creatures living together in one climate are called biomes. Check out this world biome map and find out which one you call home!

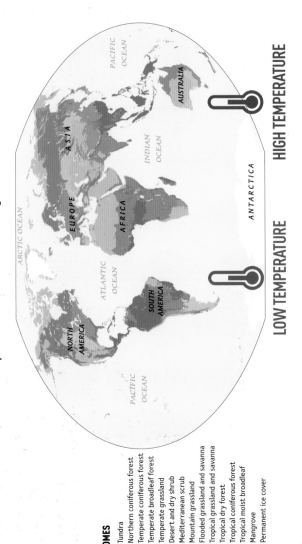

BIOMES

- Tundra
- Northern coniferous forest
- Temperate coniferous forest
- Temperate broadleaf forest
- Temperate grassland
- Desert and dry shrub
- Mediterranean scrub
- Mountain grassland
- Flooded grassland and savanna
- Tropical grassland and savanna
- Tropical dry forest
- Tropical coniferous forest
- Tropical moist broadleaf
- Mangrove
- Permanent ice cover

LOW TEMPERATURE **HIGH TEMPERATURE**

DESERT

25°F (-3.9°C)   **100°F** (37.8°C)

The desert receives just 1/10 THE AMOUNT OF RAIN that a rain forest gets! Desert air is so dry that the temperature changes dramatically between day and night, since there's no moisture in the air to trap the heat.

SHRUBLAND

91°F (32.8°C) **37°F** (2.8°C)

Shrublands are located between between **30° AND 40° NORTH AND SOUTH LATITUDE** and get less rain than forests, but more rain than deserts and grasslands. The rain is unpredictable, varying from one month to the next.

GRASSLAND

86°F (30°C) **-4°F** (-20°C)

Grasslands are found on every continent except Antarctica. Grasses range in height from **8–10 INCHES** (20–25 cm) to over **7 FEET** (2.1 m) tall. The more rainfall the grassland receives, the higher the grass grows!

TEMPERATE DECIDUOUS
FOREST

86°F (30°C) **-22°F** (-30°C)

This biome has **4 DISTINCT SEASONS**, with hot summers and cold winters.

RAIN FOREST

77°F (25°C) **68°F** (20°C)

The tropical rain forest is a hot, moist biome where it rains all year long. It is known for its dense canopies of vegetation that form three different layers. The top layer, or canopy, contains giant trees that grow to heights of **250 FEET** (75 m) or more.

CONIFEROUS
FOREST

68°F (20°C) **-40°F** (-40°C)

Coniferous forests can have cold, long, snowy winters. Some can also have **4–6 MONTHS** of warm, humid weather in the summer.

TUNDRA

64°F (18°C) **-40°F** (-40°C)

With average temperatures below 32°F (0°C) for **6–10 MONTHS** of the year, winters in the tundra are long, dark, and cold. It's so cold that there is a layer of permanently frozen soil called permafrost just below the surface.

THE SCOOP ON **SCORPIONS**

Living in deserts and grasslands all over the world, these scary-looking arachnids are a distant cousin of the spider! They use their stinging tails and poisonous venom to snack on insects and defend against predators. Fossils show that scorpions have been around for hundreds of millions of years, since before dinosaurs roamed the Earth. Get a grip on these surprising scorpion stats!

There are over

2,000

different species of scorpions.

If there isn't enough food, a scorpion slows its metabolism to

1/3

of its normal rate to save energy.

When a scorpion is in this state, it can survive on as little as

1 INSECT

per year.

Scorpions glow under ultraviolet light. Scientists aren't sure why!

Scorpions have

8 LEGS

just like their arachnid relatives: spiders, mites, and ticks.

A scorpion lives

3–8 YEARS

in the wild.

213

THE DEEP BLUE SEA

Oceans cover 71% of our planet's surface. Some of them are so deep that they'd cover the tallest mountains on Earth! Dive in and discover the deepest parts of our oceans.

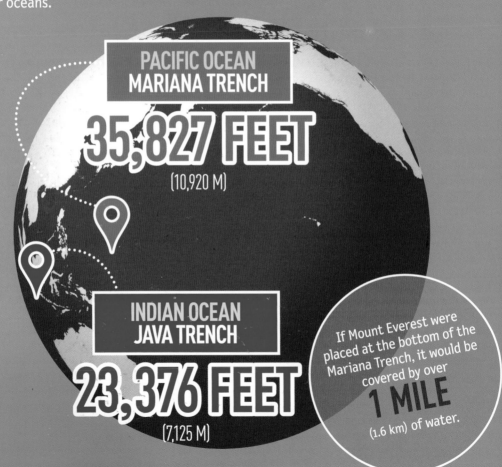

PACIFIC OCEAN
MARIANA TRENCH

35,827 FEET
(10,920 M)

INDIAN OCEAN
JAVA TRENCH

23,376 FEET
(7,125 M)

If Mount Everest were placed at the bottom of the Mariana Trench, it would be covered by over
1 MILE
(1.6 km) of water.

ARCTIC OCEAN
MOLLOY DEEP

18,599 FEET
(5,669 M)

The average ocean depth is 12,100 FEET (3,688 m).

ATLANTIC OCEAN
PUERTO RICO TRENCH

28,232 FEET
(8,605 M)

PRICE TIME TRAVELER

Wonder how much things cost 100 years ago? Grab your piggy bank, hop in our price time machine, and find out!

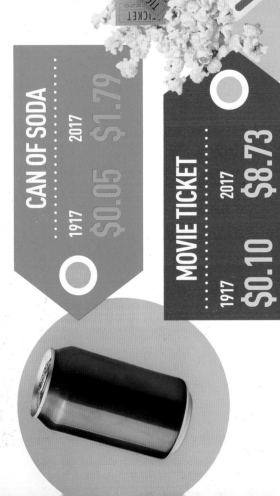

CAN OF SODA

1917 — $0.05
2017 — $1.79

MOVIE TICKET

1917 — $0.10
2017 — $8.73

1 DOZEN EGGS

1917 — $0.34
2017 — $1.68

POP CORN

TICKET

FIRST CLASS STAMP

1917 $0.02

2017 $0.49

1 GALLON (3.8 L) OF GAS

1917 $0.23

2017 $2.29

A NEW CAR

1917 $2,000

2017 $31,250

All prices listed are averages.

MAPLE MADNESS

Did you know that there are more than 865 different species of trees in the United States? This familiar foliage belongs to the most popular tree in America: the red maple! Learn more about this towering tree and find out how to spot one in your neighborhood.

NUMBER OF MAPLE TREE SPECIES:

200+

HEIGHT OF TALLEST RED MAPLE IN THE U.S.:

141 FEET (43 m)

40–60 FEET (12–18 m)

AVERAGE HEIGHT:

NUMBER OF LOBES ON A MAPLE LEAF:

5

ANNUAL GROWTH:

13–24 INCHES

(33–61 cm)

AMOUNT OF SAP IT TAKES TO MAKE 1 GALLON (3.8 L) OF MAPLE SYRUP:

40 GALLONS (151 L)

A few times a year, the moon passes between the Earth and the sun.

When that happens, the sun can be partially or even completely blocked by the moon. Read on for some facts about solar eclipses.

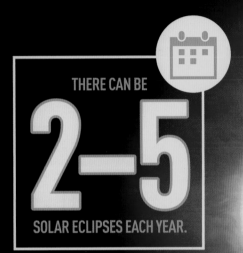

THERE CAN BE

2–5

SOLAR ECLIPSES EACH YEAR.

A TOTAL SOLAR ECLIPSE, WHERE THE MOON COMPLETELY COVERS THE SUN, CAN HAPPEN EVERY

1–2 YEARS.

SAFETY NOTE: DON'T LOOK AT THE SUN DIRECTLY DURING AN ECLIPSE! USE SPECIAL ECLIPSE GLASSES IF YOU'LL BE VIEWING A SOLAR ECLIPSE.

THE LONGEST TIME A TOTAL
SOLAR ECLIPSE CAN LAST IS

106 MINUTES.

YOU'LL BE ABLE TO SEE A
TOTAL SOLAR ECLIPSE FROM
YOUR LOCATION ONCE EVERY

375 YEARS.

THE PATH OF A TOTAL
SOLAR ECLIPSE IS ABOUT

100 MILES (160 KM)

WIDE AND CAN COVER AN AREA
OF EARTH'S SURFACE ABOUT

10,000 MILES

(16,100 KM) LONG.

WINDY CITIES

Chicago, Illinois, U.S.A., is known as the Windy City, but is it *really* the windiest city in the United States? The answer might surprise you!

What about Chicago? The Windy City's official average wind speed clocks in at

9.9 MPH
(15.9 km/h).

Average Wind Speed

| 0 MPH (0 km/h) | 5 MPH (8 km/h) | 10 MPH (16.1 km/h) | 15 MPH (24.1 km/h) |

11.8
MILES AN HOUR
(19 km/h)

12
MILES AN HOUR
(19.3 km/h)

12.2
MILES AN HOUR
(19.6 km/h)

BUFFALO, NEW YORK

CORPUS CHRISTI, TEXAS

OKLAHOMA CITY, OKLAHOMA

12.3
MILES AN HOUR
(19.8 km/h)

12.4
MILES AN HOUR
(20 km/h)

12.6
MILES AN HOUR
(20.3 km/h)

13.6
MILES AN HOUR
(21.9 km/h)

BOSTON, MASSACHUSETTS

LUBBOCK, TEXAS

ROCHESTER, MINNESOTA

AMARILLO, TEXAS

SUPERSIZED **CITIES**

All around the world, people gather in cities to live, work, and play. What's the most populated city in the world? Explore this map of the world's biggest metro areas and find out!

NEW YORK CITY, UNITED STATES
20,200,000
PEOPLE

The most densely populated city on this list? **New York City,** where all 18.6 million people are packed into just **6,720 SQUARE MILES** (17,404 sq km).

MEXICO CITY, MEXICO
21,000,000
PEOPLE

SÃO PAULO, BRAZIL
21,100,000
PEOPLE

CAIRO, EGYPT
18,800,000
PEOPLE

DELHI, INDIA
25,700,000
PEOPLE

SHANGHAI, CHINA
23,700,000
PEOPLE

TOKYO, JAPAN
38,000,000
PEOPLE

225

Think air is just air? **Think again!** Earth's atmosphere is actually made up of many different gases. Take a deep breath and check out what's in the air we breathe.

1% ARGON

21% **OXYGEN**

How many times do you breathe each day? An adult at rest breathes about **12 BREATHS PER MINUTE.**

That's **17,000 BREATHS PER DAY!**

1%

A MIX OF:

CARBON DIOXIDE

NEON

HELIUM

METHANE

KRYPTON

HYDROGEN

78%

NITROGEN

Air also contains water vapor, usually around

1%

at sea level.

A LOOK AT THE LOUVRE

Attention, art lovers! Located in Paris, France, the Louvre Museum is the largest art museum in the world, attracting over 9 million visitors each year. First built as a fortress in the late 12th century, the building has been transformed into a home for some of the world's most treasured works of art. Take a look at this landmark and learn more about what's inside.

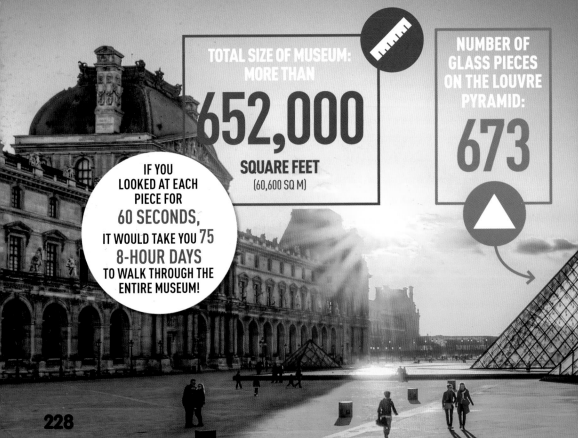

TOTAL SIZE OF MUSEUM: MORE THAN

652,000

SQUARE FEET
(60,600 SQ M)

IF YOU LOOKED AT EACH PIECE FOR **60 SECONDS,** IT WOULD TAKE YOU **75 8-HOUR DAYS** TO WALK THROUGH THE ENTIRE MUSEUM!

NUMBER OF GLASS PIECES ON THE LOUVRE PYRAMID:

673

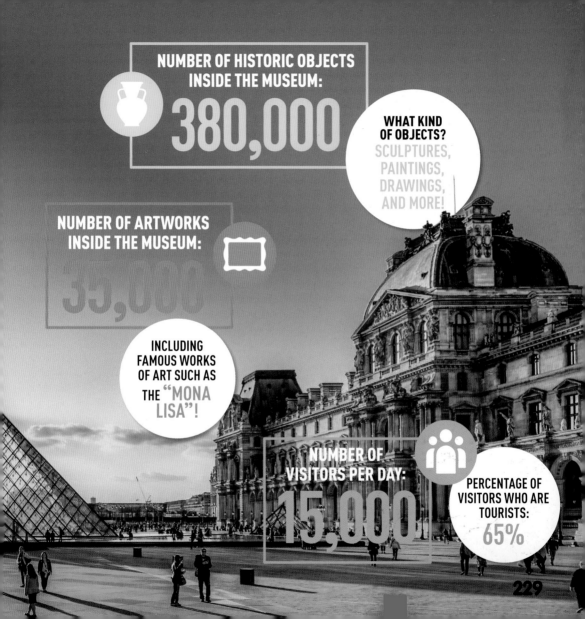

NUMBER OF HISTORIC OBJECTS INSIDE THE MUSEUM:

380,000

WHAT KIND OF OBJECTS? SCULPTURES, PAINTINGS, DRAWINGS, AND MORE!

NUMBER OF ARTWORKS INSIDE THE MUSEUM:

35,000

INCLUDING FAMOUS WORKS OF ART SUCH AS THE "MONA LISA"!

NUMBER OF VISITORS PER DAY:

15,000

PERCENTAGE OF VISITORS WHO ARE TOURISTS: 65%

229

PASS THE **POPCORN**

How does popcorn magically turn from a hard yellow kernel into a soft and crunchy snack? Here's the science behind this tasty treat.

STEP 1 THERE ARE **4** COMMON TYPES OF CORN:
SWEET, DENT, FLINT, AND **POPCORN.**

POPCORN IS THE ONLY KIND THAT POPS BECAUSE ITS HULL IS THIN ENOUGH TO BREAK OPEN WHEN HEATED.

STEP 2

EACH KERNEL OF POPCORN HAS A SMALL DROP OF WATER INSIDE. POPCORN NEEDS ABOUT

14% MOISTURE
TO POP CORRECTLY.

STEP 3 JUST ADD HEAT! WHETHER YOU USE A HOT AIR POPPER, A STOVE, OR A MICROWAVE, THE KERNEL NEEDS TO GET HOT FOR THE REACTION TO HAPPEN.

WHEN THE KERNEL REACHES **212°F** (100°C) THE WATER TURNS INTO STEAM AND CHANGES THE STARCH INSIDE THE KERNEL.

STEP 4 WHEN THE PRESSURE INSIDE THE KERNEL REACHES

135 POUNDS PER SQUARE INCH THE HULL BURSTS OPEN.
(9.49 kg/cm²)

STEP 5 STEAM IS RELEASED AND THE SOFT STARCH INSIDE THE KERNEL FLIPS INSIDE OUT. A KERNEL OF POPCORN CAN GET

40–50 TIMES

BIGGER AFTER IT COOKS!

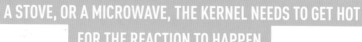

GARDEN SMACKDOWN

Look closely and you'll see lots of pretty bugs flying around your garden. Let's compare two of the most colorful creatures you might find: the monarch butterfly and the ladybug!

MONARCH BUTTERFLY

WEIGHT: .0095–.026 OUNCE (.27–.75 G)

TYPE: INSECT

DIET: HERBIVORE

LIFE SPAN: 6–8 MONTHS

SIZE: 3.7–4.1 INCH WINGSPAN (9.4–10.5 CM)

NUMBER OF WINGS: 2

NUMBER OF LEGS: 6

NUMBER OF ANTENNAE: 2

MONARCHS CAN TRAVEL UP TO **3,000 MILES** (4,828 KM) DURING THEIR YEARLY MIGRATION TO A WARMER CLIMATE.

LADYBUG

WEIGHT:

.07 OUNCE (2 G)

TYPE:

BEETLE

DIET:
OMNIVORE

LIFE SPAN:
2–3 YEARS

SIZE: (8–10 MM)
0.3–0.4 INCH

NUMBER OF WINGS:
2

NUMBER OF LEGS:
6

NUMBER OF ANTENNAE:
2

One ladybug can eat up to 5,000 insects in its lifetime! Their favorite snack? Aphids!

THE NUMBER OF SPOTS ON A LADYBUG VARIES BY SPECIES, BUT THE MOST COMMON KIND OF LADYBUG IN NORTH AMERICA HAS 7 SPOTS.

COOL

EXT

234

RAS!

How We MADE IT

Infographics might seem simple at first, but each part—whether it's a photo, illustration, or number—has been carefully designed so that it tells the story in a simple yet accurate way. Here's how we made these cool infographics in *By the Numbers 3.14*.

DELICIOUS DOUGHNUT DATA

Whether they're glazed, iced, sprinkled, or filled, people around the world love doughnuts! Researchers surveyed 735 people in the United States to find out their favorite flavors. Get ready to be a-glazed! Er ... amazed!

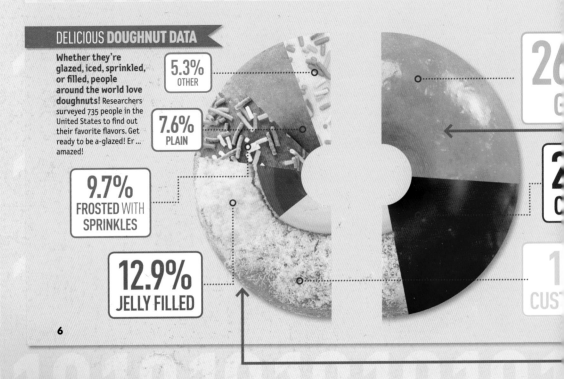

5.3%
OTHER

7.6%
PLAIN

9.7%
FROSTED WITH SPRINKLES

12.9%
JELLY FILLED

26
G

2
C

1
CUST

6

236

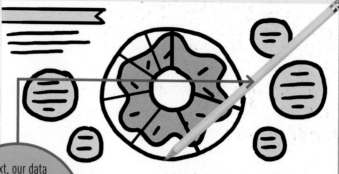

Each piece starts the same way: with fascinating facts! Our researchers combed through lots of scientific sources, studies, and surveys to find this delicious doughnut data.

Next, our data designers start sketching. These quick drawings help us test different design ideas and find the best way to show the data.

Now that we've found our information and our design idea, we can get started on the graphics. Because this data is about doughnuts, we used these mouthwatering photos to help tell the story. Designing this infographic is making us a little hungry. Maybe it's time for a snack break!

Our infographic looks good enough to eat, but we need to make sure that it's accurate, too. Every infographic in this book was reviewed by a data expert. In this pie chart, each "slice" was checked to make sure that, for example, the chocolate doughnut slice really does make up 20.8% of the whole pie chart shape.

Once our chart is finished, we add big numbers and helpful lines to make the chart easier to read and understand.

8%
ZED

8%
OLATE

%
FILLED

7

Create your own INFOGRAPHIC
Here's how to MAKE YOUR NUMBERS POP!

Feeling inspired by the incredible images in this book? You can make your own! Skip the boring old bar chart and make your next math or science project unforgettable with a cool information graphic (infographic)—just like the ones you've seen here! To make your numbers pop off the page in an interesting way, don't miss these tips from a National Geographic designer. You'll be making your own amazing infographics in no time!

FIND YOUR FACTS

The first step to any successful infographic is a **solid set of data.** Search through books, newspapers, or the Internet to find interesting facts. Infographics are the most interesting when they **answer a question, tell a story, or share a surprise.** Do you see any patterns, insights, or funny facts hidden in the numbers?

COMPARE AND CONTRAST

Now that you've found your numbers, it's time to make them **easier to understand.** Let's say you found a fact that says there are 1,600,000 cows living in South Dakota. That sounds like a lot of cows, but when you **compare** that number to the amount of people living there—853,175—you realize that there are twice as many cows as people. **Now that's a fun fact!**

DESIGN THE DATA

You've seen lots of different infographics in this book. So which type should you choose for your piece? That depends on the data! Are you showing different parts of a whole? Use a pie chart. Do you have information from lots of places on the globe? Try plotting the points on a map. Need more ideas? Check out pages 4–5 to read more about the many styles of infographics we used in this book.

THINK IN PICTURES

Here's where the graphics part comes in! How can you use pictures, drawings, and icons to tell your story? Striking visuals, fun colors, and cool illustrations will make your data come to life. Not only will your infographic be fun to look at, but it'll help your audience understand your point of view, too.

ADD THE DETAILS

Don't forget the details! Add labels, keys, lines, icons, and text to help your readers digest the data.

SHARE FUN FACTS

There are so many fascinating facts out there! Throughout this book, we've included little tidbits that add more to the story. You can use fun-fact bubbles to share interesting information you've discovered along the way. That's how to make your infographic truly unforgettable!

MAKE IT YOURS!

It's your infographic, so make it unique! The only limit is your own creativity. Use all different shapes and sizes, styles, and colors. Use your personality and style to grab the reader's attention. If you have fun making it, you can guarantee that everyone will have fun reading it!

Want MORE?

Dive deeper into the world of infographics! Together with a parent, check out these great resources to find out more about data and design, plus learn some awesome new facts along the way.

IN PRINT

Cabot, Tom. *The Infographic Guide to Science.* Richmond Hill: Firefly Books, 2016.

Cook, Gareth, ed. *The Best American Infographics 2016.* New York: Houghton Mifflin Harcourt, 2016.

D'Efilippo, Valentina, and James Ball. *The Infographic History of the World.* Richmond Hill: Firefly Books, 2013.

Krum, Randy. *Cool Infographics: Effective Communication With Data Visualization and Design.* Hoboken: Wiley, 2013.

Martineau, Susan, and Vicky Barker. *Infographics for Kids.* Watertown: Charlesbridge, 2016.

Yikun, Liu, and Dong Zhao, ed. *Visual Storytelling: Infographic Design in News.* Victoria: The Images Publishing Group, 2016.

Wiedemann, Julius, ed. *National Geographic Infographics.* Cologne: Taschen, 2016.

Google Trends

trends.google.com

Need to know what's trending? Find out what people are searching for on the web with Google Trends—and get some ideas for your next infographic project!

Infogram

infogr.am

This website makes infographics like magic! Just input your numbers and watch as the program draws the data before your very eyes.

Piktochart

piktochart.com

You don't have to be a professional designer to make infographics with this cool tool. Grab a parent and use this free resource to bring your infographics to life.

United States Government Open Data

data.gov

If you're wondering where to find interesting data for your own designs, look no further! Check out this gold mine of free data about topics like weather, nature, energy, science, and more.

Visme

visme.co

With a parent's help, use this free online infographics maker to create your own charts, graphs, and more using hundreds of beautiful templates.

By the Numbers 3.14
SOURCES AND NOTES

Frequent Flyers
Pages 8–9
Airports Council International. "Year To Date Passenger Traffic." aci.aero/Data-Centre/Monthly-Traffic-Data/Passenger-Summary/Year-to-date.

Superhero Stats
Pages 12–13
Guinness Book of World Records. "Marvel's Deadpool Wedding Issue Makes Comic Book History." guinnessworldrecords.com/news/2014/4/marvel-breaks-record-for-most-comic-book-characters-on-a-cover-with-deadpool-wedding-issue-56656.

Box Office Mojo. "Comic Book Adaptation Box Office Figures." boxofficemojo.com/genres/chart/?id=comicbookadaptation.htm.

Super Spellers
Pages 16-17
National Spelling Bee. "National Spelling Bee Statistics." Accessed May 1, 2016. spellingbee.com/statistics.

The Big Picture
Pages 18-19
Heyman, Stephen. "Photos, Photos Everywhere." The New York Times, July 29, 2015, accessed March 2, 2017. nytimes.com/2015/07/23/arts/international/photos-photos-everywhere.html?_r=0.

Cell Phone Numbers
Pages 20-21
Duggan, Maeve. "Cell Phone Activities 2013." Pew Research Center, September 19, 2013, accessed March 2, 2017. pewinternet.org/2013/09/19/cell-phone-activities-2013.

How Many Pennies?
Pages 28-29
United States Mint. "Production & Sales Figures: Circulating Coins." competition.usmint.gov/circulating-coins-production-figures.

Snowboarding With Shaun
Pages 30-31
Laskow, Sarah. "Snowboarding Was Almost Called 'Snurfing'." The Atlantic, October 13, 2014, accessed March 2, 2017. theatlantic.com/technology/archive/2014/10/snowboarding-was-almost-called-snurfing/381308.

Snowsports Industries America. "2015 SIA Snow Sports Fact Sheet." snowsports.org/research-surveys/snow-sports-fact-sheet.

X Games. "Shaun White X Games Competition History." xgames.espn.com/xgames/athletes/3014000/shaun-white.

Turn Up the Tunes
Pages 42-43
Billboard. "Greatest Of All Time: Hot 100 Songs." billboard.com/charts/greatest-hot-100-singles.

Favorite Sport Stats
Pages 46-47
The Aspen Institute Project Play. "State Of Play 2016 Report." aspenprojectplay.org/sites/default/files/StateofPlay_2016_FINAL.pdf.

Sleepy Babies
Pages 48-49
National Sleep Foundation. "How Many Hours Do Dogs Sleep Each Day?" sleep.org/articles/how-much-do-dogs-sleep.

Stanford Children's Health. "Newborn-Sleep Patterns." stanfordchildrens.org/en/topic/default%3Fid%3Dnewborn-sleep-patterns-90-P02632&sa=U&ei=58e3VM6CIlr5yATNnIGwAg&ved=0CG8QFjAT&usg=AFQjCNFvyKhlh5_8yFZvCBirEv-fTY56pQ.

Blast Off!
Pages 52-53
National Aeronautics and Space Administration. "What Was The Saturn V?" nasa.gov/audience/forstudents/5-8/features/nasa-knows/what-was-the-saturn-v-58.html.

Heartbeats
Pages 56-57
San Jose State University. "Animal Longevity and Scale." sjsu.edu/faculty/watkins/longevity.htm.

Favorite Food Facts
Pages 66-67
Caine-Bish, N. and Scheule, B. 2007. Food Preferences of School Age Children and Adolescents in an Ohio School District. Journal of Child Nutrition & Management. docs.schoolnutrition.org/newsroom/jcnm/07fall/caine-bish/index.asp.

Now That's a Big Rig
Pages 68-69
Berg, Phil. "10 Things You Didn't Know About Semi Trucks." Popular Mechanics, August 8, 2012, accessed March 2, 2017. popularmechanics.com/cars/trucks/g116/10-things-you-didnt-know-about-semi-trucks.

Fast Food Habits
Pages 74-75
Gallup. "Fast Food Still Major Part of U.S. Diet." gallup.com/poll/163868/fast-food-major-part-diet.aspx.

Scott's Year In Space
Pages 76-77
National Aeronautics and Space Administration. "One-Year Mission." nasa.gov/1ym.

Huge Hailstone
Pages 82-83
Insurance Institute for Business & Home Safety. "Hail Facts." disastersafety.org/wp-content/uploads/Hail-Facts_IBHS.pdf.

National Aeronautics and Space Administration. "Precipitation Education: How Does Hail Form?" pmm.nasa.gov/education/content/how-does-hail-form.

Racing Roller Coaster
Pages 90-91
Six Flags. "Six Flags Great Adventure & Safari Attractions: Kingda Ka." sixflags.com/greatadventure/attractions/kingda-ka.

100 Years Of Names
Pages 92-93
United States Social Security Administration. "Top Names Over the Last 100 Years." ssa.gov/oact/babynames/decades/century.html.

Soda Pop Sayings
Pages 94-95
McConchie, Alan. "Pop vs. Soda Statistics." popvssoda.com/statistics/ALL.html.

Celestial Counts
Pages 96-97
Choi, Charles Q. "Solar System Facts: A Guide to Things Orbiting Our Sun." Space.com, January 22, 2016, accessed March 2, 2017. space.com/56-our-solar-system-facts-formation-and-discovery.html.

Filling Up With Fuel
Pages 98-99
International Energy Agency. "Key World Energy Statistics 2016." iea.org/publications/freepublications/publication/key-world-energy-statistics.html.

Great Gourds
Pages 106–107
Ott, Cindy. *Pumpkin: The Curious History of an American Icon*. Seattle: University of Washington Press, 2012.

Penn State University Extension. "Pumpkin Production." extension.psu.edu/business/ag-alternatives/horticulture/melons-and-pumpkins/pumpkin-production.

Radical Readers
Pages 110-111
Scholastic. "Kids & Family Reading Report." scholastic.com/readingreport.

A Very Quick Trip
Pages 118-119
University of Maryland. "Astronomical Distances." janus.astro.umd.edu/astro/distance.

Amazing Maize
Pages 120-121
National Corn Growers Association. "World of Corn Report 2016." ncga.com/upload/files/documents/pdf/publications/WOC-2016.pdf.

Candy Colors
Pages 122–123
Heckard, Robert F. and Utts, Jessica M. *Mind on Statistics*. Boston: Cengage Learning, 2014.

America's Favorite Felines
Pages 124-125
Cat Fanciers Association. "The Cat Fanciers' Association Announces Most Popular Breeds for 2014." cfa.org/AboutCFA/News/PressReleases/PressRelease20150216Top10Breeds.aspx.

Climate Crisis
Pages 138-139
United States Environmental Protection Agency. "Sources of Greenhouse Gas Emissions." epa.gov/ghgemissions/sources-greenhouse-gas-emissions.

Climbing Kilimanjaro
Pages 146-147
Climb Kilimanjaro Guide. "Swiss Sets New Kilimanjaro Fastest Ascent and Descent Record." climbkilimanjaroguide.com/kilimanjaro-fastest-ascent.

Pasta Power
Pages 148-149
International Pasta Organization. "History of Pasta." internationalpasta.org/index.aspx?id=6.

National Pasta Association. "Fun Facts." ilovepasta.org/public/fun-facts.

Save the Bees, Please!
Pages 150-151
Greenpeace. "Save The Bees." greenpeace.org/usa/sustainable-agriculture/save-the-bees.

Tourist To-Do List
Pages 156-157
Travel and Leisure. "World's Most Visited Tourist Attractions." travelandleisure.com/slideshows/worlds-most-visited-tourist-attractions.

Giant General Sherman
Pages 160-161
United States National Park Service. "The General Sherman Tree." nps.gov/seki/learn/nature/sherman.htm.

Thirst Quenchers
Pages 162-163
United States Centers for Disease Control. "Beverage Consumption Among High School Students, United States, 2010." cdc.gov/mmwr/preview/mmwrhtml/mm6023a2.htm.

Cattle Call
Pages 164-165
United States Department of Agriculture. "National Agricultural Statistics Service." quickstats.nass.usda.gov.

Go Ask Google
Pages 168-169
Google Trends. "Year In Search 2015." trends.google.com/trends/topcharts#vm=cat&geo=US&date=2015&cid.

Wide Wingspans
Pages 170-171
United States Department of the Interior Fish and Wildlife Service. "California Condor Recovery Program." fws.gov/cno/es/pdf%20files/Ca-Condor-Recovery-Prog2015PopulationStatus.pdf.

Hot and Cold
Pages 174-175
Arizona State University. "World Meteorological Organization Global Weather & Climate Extremes Archive." wmo.asu.edu/content/world-meteorological-organization-global-weather-climate-extremes-archive.

Animated A-Listers
Pages 184-185
Box Office Mojo. "Animated Movies at the Box Office." Accessed May 1, 2016. boxofficemojo.com/genres/chart/?id=animation.htm.

Veggie Values
Pages 188-189
Caine-Bish, N. and Scheule, B. 2007. Food Preferences of School Age Children and Adolescents in an Ohio School District. *Journal of Child Nutrition & Management*. docs.schoolnutrition.org/newsroom/jcnm/07fall/caine-bish/index.asp.

Pie Charts
Pages 202-203
Epicurious. "America's Favorite Pies." epicurious.com/archive/blogs/editor/2008/04/americas-favori.html.

The Perfect PB&J
Pages 208-209
Thomson, Julie R. "The Perfect Equation For The Ultimate Peanut Butter And Jelly Sandwich." *Huffington Post*, September 9, 2014, accessed March 2, 2017. huffingtonpost.com/2014/09/08/best-peanut-butter-and-jelly-sandwich_n_5767788.html.

Biome Basics
Pages 210-211
National Aeronautics and Space Administration Earth Observatory. "Mission: Biomes." earthobservatory.nasa.gov/Experiments/Biome/index.php.

Windy Cities
Pages 222-223
Erdman, Jon. "America's Windiest Cities." Weather.com, March 16, 2016, accessed March 2, 2017. weather.com/tv/shows/amhq/news/10-windiest-large-cities-america-20140408#/11.

Super Sized Cities
Pages 224-225
United Nations Department of Economic and Social Affairs, Population Division. "World Population." esa.un.org/unpd/wpp.

Air Recipe
Pages 226-227
National Aeronautics and Space Administration. "Earth Fact Sheet." nssdc.gsfc.nasa.gov/planetary/factsheet/earthfact.html.

Pass The Popcorn
Pages 230-231
The Popcorn Board. "What Makes Popcorn Pop?" popcorn.org/Facts-Fun/What-Makes-Popcorn-Pop.

INDEX

Boldface indicates illustrations.

PHOTO CREDITS

Since 1888, the National Geographic Society has funded more than 12,000 research, exploration, and preservation projects around the world. The Society receives funds from National Geographic Partners, LLC, funded in part by your purchase. A portion of the proceeds from this book supports this vital work. To learn more, visit natgeo.com/info.

For more information, visit nationalgeographic.com, call 1-800-647-5463, or write to the following address:

National Geographic Partners, LLC
1145 17th Street N.W.
Washington, D.C. 20036-4688 U.S.A.

Visit us online at nationalgeographic.com/books

For librarians and teachers: ngchildrensbooks.org

More for kids from National Geographic:
kids.nationalgeographic.com

For information about special discounts for bulk purchases, please contact National Geographic Books Special Sales: specialsales@natgeo.com

For rights or permissions inquiries, please contact National Geographic Books Subsidiary Rights: bookrights@natgeo.com

Editorial, Design, and Production by Jennifer Adrion and Omar Noory of These Are Things

Art Direction and Cover Design by Julide Dengel

The publisher wishes to thank everyone who helped make this book possible: Ariane Szu-Tu, editor; Sarah Mock, senior photo editor; Sally Abbey, managing editor; Joan Gossett, editorial production manager; Alix Inchausti, production editor; Anne LeongSon and Gus Tello, design production assistants.

Trade paperback ISBN: 978-1-4263-2865-7
Reinforced library binding ISBN: 978-1-4263-2866-4

Printed in China
17/PPS/1

Why 8 is GREAT!

NATIONAL GEOGRAPHIC KiDS

awesome **8** eXtreme

8 EPIC OLYMPIC MOMENTS

8 DANGERS OF NATURE

8 COLORFUL CORNERS OF THE EARTH

8 PIECES OF AMAZING ART

8 AWE-INSPIRING SIGHTS IN AFRICA

50 picture-packed top 8 lists!

JEN AGRESTA & SARAH WASSNER FLYNN

TOP 8:

MONSTER FISH, OVER-THE-TOP TOYS, SPOOKY GHOST TOWNS . . . discover the Top 8 coolest things on the planet in all kinds of quirky categories in this awesome visual list book.

Which bed do you want to crawl into?

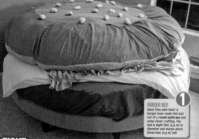

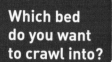

EIGHT
OUT-OF-THE-BOX **BEDS**
FROM KOOKY KINGS TO QUIRKY QUEENS, CHECK OUT SOME OF THE WEIRDEST PLACES TO REST YOUR HEAD. SWEET DREAMS!

1 BURGER BED
Want fries with that? A burger lover made this bed out of a **round mattress** and some clever crafting. The bed is eight feet (2.4 m) in diameter and about three feet (0.9 m) tall.

2 PERFECT POD
Travel may make you weary, but rest assured that you'll be able to fight jet lag with a quick snooze in a **sleep pod**. Popping up at major airports, these capsules can be booked by the hour, allowing you a private—and silent—spot to squeeze in a catnap.

3 IN THE FOLD
Why throw out old cardboard boxes away when you can sleep on it? That's the idea behind this **bed made from cardboard** folded in an intricate accordionlike design. The best part? You can compact it in a snap, making it easy to take your bed from one sleeping spot to another.

4 DRIVE TIME
Cruise into a good night's sleep in one of the unique automotive-themed rooms at the V8 Hotel in Stuttgart, Germany. In this retro bed—a converted Cadillac Coupe de Ville—you can snooze under a starry sky at the drive-in cinema.

5 FEATHER YOUR NEST
Snuggle up in this **circular, nature-inspired bed** and you'll be as cozy as a baby bird. With giant, soft pillows and a wide space for snuggling, this is one nest you might never want to leave.

6 SOFT BALL
Fabric-covered balls make up this **bumpy bed**. Though it may not look comfy, the supersoft beds are actually designed to adjust to your body position as you move around, allowing you to sink into a deep and peaceful sleep.

EACH BED FEATURES 120 BALLS LINED WITH ELASTIC BANDS, MAKING IT FLEXIBLE ENOUGH TO FOLD INTO ANY POSITION.

7 BRANCHING OUT
You'll really go out on a limb when you sleep on this **four-poster bed**. Handcrafted out of iron, each post resembles a thin tree trunk, their branches meeting in the middle to support a bird's nest. Want one of your own? Better start saving. These tree beds start at $20,500.

COST FOR ONE OF THE WORLD'S MOST EXPENSIVE BEDS? $175,000 (US)

8 SO TWISTED
Give your sleepy time a twist by lying down on this **spiral-shaped mattress**. Part of an exhibit by a team of Calan artists, this bed is said to represent the often-twisted and strange connection between sleep and dreams.

36 37

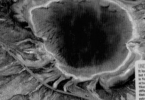

Which of these seems the scariest?

EIGHT
DANGERS OF NATURE
IF LOOKS COULD KILL ... SOMETIMES NATURE IS BEST ADMIRED FROM A DISTANCE.

1 UNDER THE RAINBOW
It looks like a rainbow hot tub, but the **Grand Prismatic Spring** in Yellowstone National Park is actually a scalding pool of acid. Yikes! Its varying colors represent different habitats for bacteria that have mastered life in an extreme environment.

2 FATAL FROGGIES
In tropical forests of Central and South America, touching **poison dart frogs** can put you in the hospital—or worse! Scientists believe these frogs become toxic as a result of eating ants, beetles, and termites that carry plant poisons.

WHEN TOXIC CREATURES USE BRIGHT COLORS TO WARN PREDATORS, IT'S CALLED APOSEMATISM.

3 OOOH—BURN!
Fire corals get their name not from their shape or bright colors but from the pain they can inflict on people who happen to touch them. These corals are distant relatives of jellyfish and use the same stinging cells—nematocysts—to capture prey and ward off predators.

4 [photo — boomslang close-up]
Don't count those lacy white blooms in your wildflower bouquet! Sap from the **giant hogweed** causes human skin to blister just like a third-degree burn when exposed to sunlight.

5 DEADLY BITE
Though the **boomslang** is highly venomous—one of the most venomous snakes in Africa—fewer than 10 human deaths have been recorded from their bites. It is a "rear-fanged" snake, meaning its fangs are way back in its mouth—coupled with the reptile to open its mouth to nearly 180 degrees to take a big bite. Boomslangs enjoy a diet of frogs, lizards, chameleons, birds, and mice.

6 FORBIDDEN FRUIT
These apples may look tasty, but stay away! All parts of the **manchineel tree** are poisonous, and ingesting any part of it can be deadly. Found in Florida, Mexico, Central America, and many Caribbean islands, the tree oozes a toxic sap that reportedly causes blisters when it touches the skin.

7 BLUE RINGS OF DEATH
The bottle-cap-size **blue-ringed octopus** is as cute as a button, but watch out for this little guy. It uses its sharp beak and poison just below to paralyze prey, as well as any humans who make the unfortunate mistake of picking it up near swimming beaches in Australia.

8 SERIOUS STINGER
Beneath what looks like a 'armless' iridescent bubble lies the **Portuguese man-of-war's** dangerous weapon: stinging tentacles that extend an average of 30 feet (10 m). They work like a dragnet to snare krill and small fish—or an unfortunate swimmer's arm or leg. Watch where you swim!

98 99

Ever wondered what a really **TINY INFOGRAPHIC** looks like? This square represents just **0.01%** OF THIS WHOLE PAGE!